Mass Murderers and the Seven Deadly Sins

William Timmerman, PhD

Mass Murderers and the Seven Deadly Sins

2022

Pen Shop Publishing
San Antonio, Texas

William Timmerman, PhD

Table of Contents

Introduction

"You Demean Me, I Be Mean to You!"

Demean means to discredit · to lower someone's dignity or status

A mother calls her son and tells him McDonald's employees laughed at her when she complained her french fries were cold. Her 20-year-old son comes in and shoots one of the fast-food employees dead. The mother told the New York Post, "My son is just saying that he gotta do what he gotta do…" This is an example of "You demean me, I be mean to you!" In this case, his mother was demeaned in his mind, so he defended his mother's honor by shooting someone which most sane people would say was crazy thinking. A customer at a McDonald's in Georgia has been arrested after allegedly spitting on one employee and shooting another during an argument that ensued at the pick-up window that had to include french fries. A woman in St. Louis County, Missouri, is accused of shooting a McDonald's employee after a dispute over a french fry discount coupon. What is it about McDonald's french fries? And what is it about this crazy world that when people now feel demeaned, they go overboard in their reaction and heap violence on the perceived perpetrator. It goes way beyond an "eye for an eye, a tooth for a tooth" mentality. "You deny me my fries or give me cold ones, I shoot you!"

The "eye for an eye" commandment in Exodus 21:23–27 means a person who has injured another person is to be penalized to a similar degree by the injured party. As Wikipedia states: "The intent behind the principle was to restrict compensation to the value of the loss." A "You deny me my fries or give me cold ones, I shoot you!" seems like a serious "overkill" (pardon the expression) penalty for a mistake or error by the McDonald's employees.

As Fr. Mark Goring likes to say, "The world is going bonkers." Boy, is he ever right. Here are more examples of the pandemic of hate and violence in our world.

"More than 10,000 people reported to law enforcement last year that they were the victim of a hate crime because of their race or ethnicity, sexual orientation, gender, religion or disability – a number that has been on the rise in recent years, according to FBI's annual hate crime statistics report" (CNN, October 26, 2021). The Center for the Study of Hate and Extremism reports that hate crimes in major cities rose in the first half of 2022, following double-digit increases over the past two years. At least nine states broke annual records in 2021.

<blockquote>"Why is there so much madness in our world? Why can't we stop it? Why do we hate others?"
-Dababish Mrdiha</blockquote>

Road rage incidents have become commonplace in today's America. The most common types of road rage are tailgating, yelling curse words, or honking at another vehicle or giving them the finger are factors in more than half of all fatal crashes. According to AAA, in 2019, almost 80% of drivers admitted to significant anger, aggression, or road rage within the last 30 days while driving. "78% of drivers reported that they had engaged in at least one aggressive driving behavior within the last year." Why? Because Inconsiderate drivers offended them in their mind. In a seven-year period, road rage incidents caused 218 murders and 12,610 injuries.

Mass shootings now occur more frequently in our country than ever before. Wikipedia states "Between 1982 and 2011, a mass shooting occurred roughly once every 200 days. However, between 2011 and 2014, that rate has accelerated greatly with at least one mass shooting occurring every 64 days in the United States." According to some experts, the shooters simply want attention. They believe they have no meaning or importance and want "to stand out" in the crowd or get even with people for demeaning them. It is why they try to gain a larger head count and try and outdo the last mass shooting to gain public recognition.

In 1999, 12th grade students Eric Harris and Dylan Klebold murdered 12 of their classmates, a teacher and twenty-four injured at Columbine High School in Colorado. It was the deadliest high school shooting in U.S. history at the time. Experts believe the shooting has since inspired dozens of copycat killings, known as the Columbine effect. The FBI and its team of psychiatrists and psychologists have offered their explanations of why the two killers did what they did. In Dave Cullen's article The Depressive and the Psychopath, Slate, April 2004, Klebold was the "depressive; Harris the "psychopath." FBI lead Columbine investigator Dwayne Fuselier, a clinical psychologist, said, "Klebold was hurting inside while Harris wanted to hurt people." Harris' private journal was filled with contempt and disgust for "the morons" around him. Dr. Robert Hare, another psychologist consulted by the FBI about Columbine, said Harris' private journal contained the rantings of someone with a messianic-grade superiority complex, out to punish the entire human race for its appalling inferiority. "I feel like God and I wish I was, having everyone being OFFICIALLY lower than me. I already know that I am higher than most anyone in the f…… welt [world] in terms of universal Intelligence." It may look like hate, but "It's more about demeaning other people," Hare said.

Here we find a reverse twist on the word "demean" or "demeaning." People are an object of disgust for Harris. Cullen concludes about Harris, "He was a brilliant killer without a conscience, searching for the most diabolical scheme imaginable." Remember the word "diabolical" as we dig deeper into why there is so much violence in the world today.

We Live in a Violent World

"The Lord examines the righteous, but the wicked, those who love violence, he hates with a passion"- Psalm 11:5

The prophet Habakkuk lived around 600 B.C. This comes from the first part of his short book in the Old Testament.

"How long, O LORD? I cry for help
but you do not listen!
I cry out to you, "Violence!"
but you do not intervene.
Why do you let me see ruin;
why must I look at misery?
Destruction and violence are before me;
there is strife, and clamorous discord"-1 Habakkuk 1:2-3

Conditions back in Habakkuk's time were not unlike what we face in today's world. In addition to school shootings, road rage, mass murders and wars are always going on some place in the world. The news is also filled with accounts of workplace violence, at sporting events, and seemingly never-ending cases of domestic violence and child abuse.

Recently at least 131 people died after a soccer game riot in Indonesia. Irate fans stormed the field mad at their own team for losing the match when the police tear-gassed people in the stadium leading the crowd to a stampede which caused all the deaths along with many more injured. How dare their team lose! They attacked them for the mistake of losing the game to a lesser team.

Baseball unlike soccer, rugby, football, or boxing is not considered a violent sport but pitchers at times will throw a "beanball" at a hitter as a violent act often in retaliation. Some batters have been hit in the face or their head and had their careers shortened or derailed because of it. Ray Chapman died from getting struck in the head. Tony Conigliaro was hit in the eye, and his vision later deteriorated to the point where he was forced to retire. Pitchers today often throw fastball pitches at 98 to 100 miles an hour that when aimed at a batter's "bean" or head can cause serious damage or death.

Workplace violence is frequently in the news. In 2021, a 19-year-old former employee shot and killed nine people and injured seven others at a FedEx Ground facility in Indianapolis, Indiana. During a press conference with Japanese Prime Minister Yoshihide Suga, President Biden decried the recent string of mass shootings in the United States as a "national embarrassment." The FBI concluded that the mass shooting was "an act of suicidal murder" intended to "demonstrate his masculinity and capability while fulfilling a final desire to experience killing people" (see indy/star).

The "going postal" comes from a mass shooting in 1986 when United States Postal Service worker Patrick Sherrill shot a total of 20 co-workers before killing himself. Fourteen victims died in the attack which is still the deadliest among incidents of workplace violence in the United States. He reportedly was reprimanded the

day before by his supervisors for performance problems.
At least nine more shootings have involved postal workers since then. In one case, the worker shot the supervisor because he had sent him home due to intoxication, another worker for adding more deliveries to his work load, a third for too many wrong deliveries and a fourth was terminated for too many run-ins with customers.

"Over the past 10 years, more than 20,000 American children are believed to have been killed in their own homes by family members. That is nearly four times the number of US soldiers killed in Iraq and Afghanistan (BBC News, October 17, 2011). "Why is the problem of violence against children so much more acute in the US than anywhere else in the industrialized world," asks Michael Petit, President of Every Child Matters. A literature review of 23 studies indicates that 28% of girls and 17% of boys will be sexually abused before they are 18 years old (Darkness to Light).

Domestic violence is a big problem in our country. According to the National Statistics Domestic Violence Fact Sheet:

- More than 1 in 3 women and 1 in 4 men have experienced either physical violence, rape, or stalking by an intimate partner in their lifetime.
- Intimate partner violence accounts for 15% of all violent crimes annually in the United States.

Rape of females continues to be rampant. The World Population Review of 2020 reported 84,769 rapes in

America. As usual, many are not reported. Sexual lusters violently dehumanize other people especially women and children by using them as objects for their own selfish sexual pleasure. They have little to no regard for the other person's human dignity and self-worth. Christian religion teaches that sexual morality is rooted in the dignity of the human person and the goodness of human sexuality. Consequently, it condemns sexual crimes including rape, domestic abuse, incest, and child sexual abuse.

An overriding motive for committing acts of domestic and interpersonal violence in a relationship is to establish and maintain relationships based on power and control over victims. Power is a dominant motive in most acts of violence.

Gary Ridgway, also known as the Green River Killer, was convicted of 49 murders. Most of his victims were alleged to be sex workers or female underage runaways. He reportedly had a love-hate relationship with his mother. He told his defense psychologists that, as an adolescent, he had conflicting feelings of anger and sexual attraction toward his mother and fantasized about killing her (Blaine Gary).

Ridgway described the dead women he murdered as "his property" and got great satisfaction from driving past sites where he had dumped bodies and then returned to have sex with the body until putrefaction set in. "I had control of her when I killed her," he said, "and I'd have control over her where she was still in my possession." He said he had nightmares about "forgetting the locations and thus losing control of the victims" (Sandi Doughton). What is the definition of control but "the power to influence or direct people's behavior or the course of events."

The sanctity, peace and safety of churches or places of worship has been violated repeatedly in recent years. In 2015, Dylann Roof, a 21-year-old white supremacist, shot and killed nine Black worshippers including a pastor after he prayed with them for nearly an hour. Two years later in 2017, Devin Patrick Kelley killed 26 people, including an unborn child, wounded 22 others at the First Baptist Church in Sutherland Springs, Texas as the deadliest shooting in an American place of worship. According to Federal investigators Kelley was motivated by a dispute with his mother-in-law.

Libraries are supposed to be safe and quiet places yet in Clovis, New Mexico two women were killed, and four others injured including a ten-year-old boy when gunfire erupted inside a public library. The 16-year-old gunman Nathaniel Jouett was taken into custody. He had been in a fight at school several days earlier was suspended from school and decided to shoot up the library rather than the school where the fight took place. Less than 24 hours before the shooting, his girlfriend posted photos of the couple together and wrote that she was the "Luckiest girl alive… Thank you for everything you do and thank you for being in my life." He wrote, "Thank you" accompanied by a love heart. After the shooting, his girlfriend, told CNN that Jouett was distraught over what she described as a bullying incident at school on Friday (Jason Kravarik). He pleaded guilty in the shooting and was sentenced to two life sentences, with the possibility of parole, plus 40 years in prison.

After reading about all the violence in the world and especially in our country, it is only natural to ask why is this happening? There is a vast array of possible reasons in answer to the question. When the FBI was asked why serial killers do what they do, they said anger, thrill-seeking, financial gain and attention-seeking. (Morton, 2005). But what about a postal worker who shoots his coworkers, the person who rams another vehicle on purpose causing it to crash and burn, the real reason why a sixteen-year-old gunman would decide to kill people in a library rather than getting even or retaliating with the kids he fought with at school just days before? Sometimes the answer or motivation seems obvious; sometimes it is not.

THE SUN-AUGUST 12, 2019

A man murdered his five children after he realized his wife was having an affair with her toy boy lover. Timothy ______ faces the death penalty after he murdered his five children ages 8 through 1, at their home in South Carolina. He buried their bodies on a rural hillside in Alabama, days later in 2014, police said. His lawyer claimed the rampage started after he discovered his wife had embarked on an affair with their 19-year-old neighbor.

Mark David Chapman murdered John Lennon of Beatles fame on December 8, 1980. As Lennon walked into his apartment building with his wife Yoko Ono, Chapman fired five shots at Lennon from several meters away with a .38 Special revolver. Lennon was hit four times in the back. Chapman remained at the scene reading J. D. Salinger's novel The Catcher in the Rye until he was arrested by police. Lennon had signed his newly released "Double Fantasy" album for Chapman hours before Chapman shot him.

Chapman had flown from Hawaii where he had been living with his wife. He had recently read a book on Lennon and became enraged that Lennon had so much money.

In 2020, forty years after he shot and killed John Lennon, the BBC reported Chapman apologized to Lennon's wife, Yoko Ono and confessed he assassinated him because he was "extremely famous." Chapman was now famous too as a murderer.

Kens5 November 5, 2020

San Antonio police have obtained an arrest warrant for a man who is accused of slashing his love rival, possibly with a machete. Police say the suspect launched a surprise attack around 3:30 a.m. Thursday at The Jackson apartment complex, located in the 2500 block of Jackson-Keller. A preliminary report says he was armed with a machete when he went after a man who he saw leaving an apartment with his ex-girlfriend. The victim told officers he tried to back away, but the suspect still managed to cut him on his arm. He was taken to a hospital by ambulance and underwent surgery, the report said.

In these last three cases, the motives are pretty clear.

Person-Environment Fit

The author has used a version of the Person-Environment Fit model with success in the field of vocational rehabilitation for understanding a person's adjustment or maladjustment to a work environment. He decided to it use for understanding a murderer's adjustment or maladjustment to work and to other environments.

From an interactional perspective, behavior is a function of the person and the environment. Person–Environment fit (P–E fit) is the degree to which the individual's and the environmental characteristics match or do not match. Some researchers argue that it is the environment which is primarily responsible for individual behaviors, while another group of researchers believe that the personal characteristics are primarily responsible for behavior and outcomes.

The P-E fit model represents an approach to understanding the impact of the environment on the well-being and adjustment of the person as well as others in the environment. Knowing more about the characteristics of the person and the environment can provide evaluative information for the development of an intervention plan or show whether congruence or a mutual satisfaction or satisfactoriness exists. It is hoped the person–environment fit leads to positive outcomes including an overall sense of well-being.

Research on work motivation through the years has swung like a pendulum from emphasis on the person then to the environment and back again in terms of which has more power or impact or weight. It has led to questions like, "Do the keys to unlocking employee motivation lie within the environment? Or, if the answer lies more within the person, what traits are more predictive than others?" While the argument or debate over which side is more important, Person (P) or Environment (E), the model is useful in evaluating the match between the two. Here is a basic diagram showing the model:

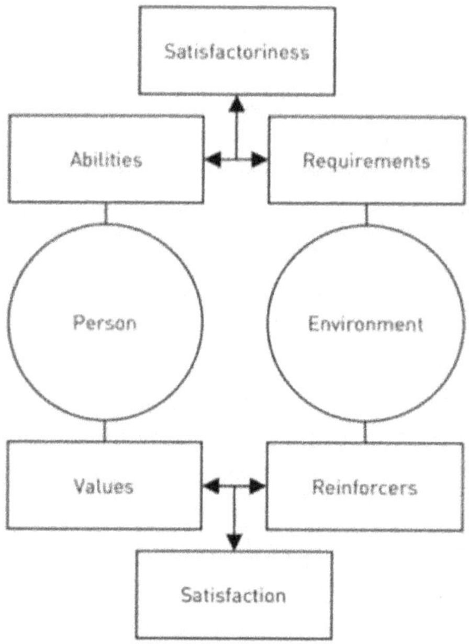

To determine the present state of a worker's adjustment to work, we start with what the person brings to the workplace or work environment. They typically bring with them abilities, skills, a work personality including their self-concept, work habits, and attitudes toward co-workers and authority figures. These will help determine their satisfactoriness from the work environment's perspective. In short, the basic requirements are: do they show up, do the work and not cause trouble? The person brings to the table their values, needs, and wants. Does the employer meet or accommodate what the employee expects or not? If so, in most cases, when the person meets the employer's requirements and expectations, they receive reinforcers in the form of pay increases, promotions, other types of recognition and hopefully sustained employment, and when all things are considered, will bring them a sense of satisfaction.

If the person is not satisfied, we are likely to have a disgruntled worker or a maladjusted worker who will either leave or cause problems in the workplace.

Generally, it "takes two to tango" in workplace shootings with the person or the employer making the first move. Poor or unsatisfactory performance frequently leads to a layoff or disciplinary action like a demotion or suspension. One shooting was due to the cut-off of the person's disability benefits, another to a pay cut. Patrick Sherrill killed thirteen post office co-workers and one of the two supervisors who had reprimanded him for poor performance the day before. The other supervisor luckily had overslept and was absent from work at the time of the shooting.

The P-E Fit model can be applied to a school setting. The person is a student. The environment consists of bricks-and-mortar, the teachers, other students or classmates, administration, and rules and expectations. Just like in a work environment, the school expects the student to "show up, do the school work and don't cause trouble." The student expects to be treated with respect, rewarded and recognized for their progress and accomplishments, and hopefully enjoys their school life with the other students.

On February 14, 2018, Valentine's Day, 19-year-old Nikolas Cruz opened fire on students and staff at Marjory Stoneman Douglas High School Parkland, Florida, and murdered 17 people and injured 17 others. Why? What were his motives? A cell phone video shows him fighting with other students a year before the Parkland school shooting. His own cell phone videos revealed that he dwelled on the Columbine killings and "studied" other mass murders which helps explain why he said, "My name is Nik, and I'm going to be the next school shooter of 2018" and "My goal is at least 20 people." Cruz then said, "It's going to be a big event," while laughing. "And when you see me on the news, you'll all know who I am." But then he added, "I am nothing, I am no one." "My life is nothing and meaningless. I live a lone life, I live in seclusion and solitude. I hate everyone and everything."

He would later say he wanted to ruin Valentine's Day for the school forever and for everybody as a way to get even with them.

Wikipedia summed up the shooter's profile this way: "In the videos, Cruz appears to describe his personal feelings, his enthusiasm and plan for the shooting, his hatred of people, and how it would make him notorious." Compare it with the FBI's statement that mass murderers are reinforced by converting their anger into wrath, enjoy the thrill-seeking it provides and the attention they receive in the public media.

Nikolas Cruz attacked the school because he felt demeaned by other students in the school environment which served to reinforce his own belief about himself: "I am nothing, I am no one."

Sometimes students believe they are being demeaned by a teacher. Two boys in Iowa allegedly beat their Spanish teacher to death with a ball bat at night while she was out walking. Although their motives have not been officially publicized pending a forthcoming trial, some fellow students revealed that the two killers were upset about the grades they received and were seen arguing with the teacher about it before her murder. "A couple of students told KCCI News they heard an argument Tuesday afternoon about trying to get a grade up in Graber's class. Not long after that, police said that the same students went to Chautauqua Park where Graber was known to go for walks." (Fairfield students say murdered teacher, student argued over grades November 5, 2021, Andrew Mollenbeck).

Columbine's killer Eric Karris' focused attention on his relationship with other students.
"Everyone is always making fun of me because of how I look...You people could have shown more respect, treated me better, asked for my knowledge or guidance more, treated me more like a senior, and maybe I wouldn't have been so ready to tear your f...... heads off. Then again, I have always hated how I looked, I make fun of people who look like me, sometimes

without even thinking sometimes just because I want to rip on myself. That's where a lot of my hate grows from. The fact that I have practically no self-esteem, especially concerning girls and looks and such."

12/29/98 I hate you people for leaving me out of so many fun things. And no don't f…… say "well that's your fault" because it isn't, you people had my phone #, and I asked and all, but no. no no
no don't let the weird looking Eric KID come along, …"

One overriding problem rises to the top after examining what these killers are trying to say. I do not fit in. People look down on me. I have low self-esteem and must do something about it. I will exert my power and receive recognition that I am an important person. Taking Dr. Seuss' famous quip "A person is a person no matter how small" and applying it to the school shooters we need to remember they are children of God even though they have done horrible, sinful things.

The core premise of P-E fit theory and the model is that stress arises not from the person or environment separately, but rather by the fit between them. It was noted earlier some researchers contend the environment has greater influence on the person than the person has on the environment. However, it depends on what the snapshot at that time in a person's life reveals. Snapshots of the early history in the life of Uvalde killer Salvador Ramos point to child-raising environmental conditions which likely would have had some negative impact on his development as a person.

A New York Post article stated his mother had a history of drug abuse and had two misdemeanors, one for theft and another for a family-violence assault and "his father was largely absent from his life." His ex-girlfriend said he told her he was sexually molested when he was a young boy by one of his mother's boyfriends. He and his mother both claimed he was repeatedly bullied in the fourth grade due to his speech impediment and in other instances. He said one time, "A student tied his shoelaces together, and he fell on his face" causing embarrassment. He said he was also kidded about wearing the same clothes day after day, which he had to do because his family could not afford new ones. With time, he missed more and more days from school and his grades suffered.

One way to react to an environment that causes too much stress for the person is to withdraw from it. He now stayed at home spending his time alone playing violent video games, becoming obsessed with school shootings and with too many moments to ruminate about school. He did not have a car or driver's license but was able to obtain the weapons and the ammunition he used to kill 19 fourth graders and two teachers in the old classroom where the reported bullying happened to him. He returned to the environment to punish it for all the negative experiences he had there.

"Ramos also hungered for fame and notoriety, according to investigators. After receiving a few views on TikTok and YouTube videos he made, Ramos bragged about being famous." If you are a nobody or worse as a subject of ridicule in a school setting, there are ways to make yourself stand out as a person of importance.

The P-E fit model has application to other situations in life including family, marriage, and child-raising. Here is a much lighter example when the environment happens to be a fairly classy restaurant.

The person, a mother, wants the family to pray aloud and make the physical gestures of Signing the Cross in public before the meal comes at the restaurant. Her husband and teenage children try to talk her out of it because of their own embarrassment in front of other people. She presents her main reasons to them. She says it is important to model a prayerful attitude for others to see and for the children to be proud of their belief in God and his blessings. In hushed voices, the teen-age daughters claim the people around them will feel uncomfortable and the waiter might have to wait until the praying is over. The older daughter then added, "Remember Mom what the bible says. 'When you pray, go into your room, close the door and pray to your Father, who is unseen.'" The mother decided to listen to her family and said the prayer before meals to herself while the family silently watched. The mother was a persistent person though.

As soon as they got home, she called a family meeting. After a civil discussion, the family arrived at a practice to try out. They can say a prayer before meals out loud together in the car before entering the restaurant which they tried out, but it did not feel right to them. The next time they went out to dinner they decided they would bow their heads and say a silent prayer together before the waiter arrived. It was still not what the mother had in mind, but she saw it as at least a good start.

The last time I saw her, she had big, broad smile on her face. Her older daughter had them join their hands together, make the Sign of the Cross, and say the prayer before meals quietly out loud at the restaurant. Like the mother, we often need to be kind, loving and patient with others to achieve mutually peaceful solutions in life.

Because the author is a Christian writer, he would be remiss if he did not introduce sin into the picture with this following fictional example of workplace violence.

Ralph, who works for a pretentious boss, must walk by this guy's brand-new black Lexus every day on the way to work and suffers with a big problem of envy. One day when things had already started off bad at home and he had been told recently that he soon was going to be laid off from work, he goes and flattens all the boss's tires. Envy leads to anger that turns into sinful wrath. As it is often said, "Anger is a normal emotion; it is what you do with it that can be the problem."

A security guard catches him and takes him off to jail. Instead of a formal layoff, he is now fired losing his unemployment compensation payments due to his firing. Once out of jail, his anger builds and builds until he decides to face the boss in the upper crust supermarket the boss patronizes. He confronts the boss pulls out a gun and shoots him. Thank God, it was only a flesh wound. He commits the horrible sin of wrath or vengeance due to total frustration and an overwhelming sense of feeling powerless.

The key words in the Ralph's story are "feeling powerless."

When an environment is too stressful for the person and they feel powerless to deal with it, mental health services can help reduce the stress so the person can manage in the environment. This story involves basically the sin of wrath.

On November 30, 2021, 15-year-old sophomore Ethan Crumbley killed four students and seven people were injured, including a teacher during a mass shooting at Oxford High School near Detroit. His journal revealed the following insights about Ethan.

One page has a drawing depicting a girl with an 'x' replacing the eyes and a semi-automatic handgun firing into the person. The words written around the drawing say "the first victim has to be pretty girl with a future so she can suffer like me."

On page 19, it reads "I will kill everyone I f****** see." Another passage on the same page reads "I will cause the biggest school shooting in Michigan's history. I have fully mentally lost it after years of fighting with my dark side. My parents won't listen to me about help or a therapist."

On page 6, it has the word "help" with bold letters colored in. Next to that, it also reads "I have zero help for my mental problems and it's causing me to shoot up the f****** school."

The prosecutors disclosed that Ethan Crumbley had hallucinations about demons and was fascinated by guns and Nazi propaganda. The day of the shooting a teacher discovered his drawing with a gun pointing at the words: "The thoughts won't stop. Help me." There was an image of a bullet with the message: "Blood everywhere."

The parents were notified to take their son home and get him into counseling within 48 hours, but the parents declined and left him stay at school.

Prosecutors in a court filing, "Put simply, they created an environment in which their son's violent tendencies flourished. They were aware their son was troubled, and then they bought him a gun."

Ethan pleaded guilty. His defense attorney Ven Johnson had this to say about the boy's home and school environments. "We will continue to fight until the truth is revealed about what went wrong leading up to this tragedy, and who, including Crumbley's parents and multiple Oxford Community Schools employees, could have and should have prevented it."

3 P's

"Shoot for the 3 P's in your life and be happy! Set your heart on the goals of power, possessions, and prestige." This is the rallying cry of secular proponents and activists in the world today where many people are relentlessly driven by dreams of success, some want to be rich, some want to be popular and applauded and some want power, prestige, and social standing. Bishop Anthony Taylor speaks about the four P's adding "pleasure" to the list. He calls the four P's the "Pernicious P's." The world tantalizes us with things, power, lust, and honor. It is the same bait used by the Devil, the prince of the world, to bury us in a life of sin he tried to use with Jesus in the desert.

"The heart wants what it wants," Woody Allen said. What does your heart want, what does my heart want? In short, what do we love? "The heart forms itself according to what it loves" (Blessed Theresa Gerhardinger). What do we spend so much our time thinking and dreaming about that consumes most of our energy, and we throw our money at? "For where your treasure is, there your heart will be also" (Matthew 6:21). The mind takes it shape from what it rests upon.

Of the four pernicious P's, power and prestige are the strongest motives leading to violence and vengeance. In the fictional story, Ralph felt powerless, so he did something about it. It did not turn out well for him in the end. As we noted earlier, mass murderers and serial killers demonstrate their power in order to bring them recognition. "You can't ignore this!" They copy-cat previous massacres and try to outdo them so everybody will now know that they exist as important people. You have demeaned me, I will now be mean to you. "Hey, look at me, now!"

Sometimes a serial killer will find a strange and possibly demonic method to have their victim's remains bring them a sense of power. Jeffrey Dahmer murdered and dismembered seventeen men and boys. Park Dietz, a forensic psychiatrist, noted that Dahmer strongly identified with the villains of The Exorcist III and Return of the Jedi, particularly the level of power they held. Dahmer had planned to build an altar in his home comprised of the skulls of some of his victims. When asked about the altar, he said it would be a "place for meditation," from where he believed he could "draw a sense of power" (Brian Masters).

As we saw earlier, Gary Ridgeway used power or "control" to obtain and keep his "possessions" of dead bodies.

Possessions

We have heard "power corrupts" and "money is power." Pope Francis called the "unfettered pursuit of money" the "dung of the devil." There is nothing inherently wrong with the possession of wealth. But as Joyce Meyer claimed, "Satan can control you if you let outward things determine your security."

Gospel writers Matthew, Mark, and Luke each tell of Jesus' warning about being rich. "Truly I tell you, it is hard for someone who is rich to enter the kingdom of heaven. Again I tell you, it is easier for a camel to go through the eye of a needle than for someone who is rich to enter the kingdom of God." (Matthew 19:23-24).

The story of "The Rich Man and Lazarus" in Luke 16:19-31 is a fitting example.

"There was a rich man who dressed in purple garments and fine linen and dined sumptuously each day. And lying at his door was a poor man named Lazarus, covered with sores, who would gladly have eaten his fill of the scraps that fell from the rich man's table. Dogs even used to come and lick his sores. When the poor man died, he was carried away by angels to the bosom of Abraham. The rich man also died and was buried, and from the netherworld, where he was in torment, he raised his eyes and saw Abraham far off and Lazarus at his side. And he cried out, 'Father Abraham, have pity on me. Send Lazarus to dip the tip of his finger in water and cool my tongue, for I am suffering torment in these flames.' Abraham replied, 'My child, remember that you received what was good during your lifetime while Lazarus likewise received what was bad; but now he is comforted here, whereas you are tormented."

Bernard" Bernie" Madoff was a fraudster financier who ran the largest Ponzi scheme in history, worth about $64.8 billion, died recently. Many of his clients were rich people who "got taken" by Bernie's get richer scheme because they were blinded by their own pursuit of possessions and the power, pleasure, and prestige that money can buy.

Jesus confronted the money changers and those selling sacrificial animals in the temple. He made a whip of cords and drove them out saying, "It is written, 'My house will be called a house of prayer,' but you are making it 'a den of robbers'" (Matthew 21:13). Because Jewish law required a temple tax of a half-shekel, Jews and visitors from other nations came to pay their taxes when they offered their sacrifices. But foreign coins with the likeness of pagan emperors like Julius Caesar would not be accepted in God's temple. So, money changers exchanged those foreign coins for Jewish money, but they did so at an exorbitant profit. Caiaphas, the high priest at the time of Jesus, was in charge of the temple, so he was quite aware of the money changers and animal sellers who were driven out by Jesus (John 2:14-16). Chances are good that he was receiving a kickback from the animal sellers and money changers as one more reason for having Jesus killed. The priests, responsible for certifying that the animals were free of defects and were paid for it, were not happy with Jesus either.

Prestige through Possessions and Riches

Will Smith sums up the challenge of pursuing recognition and prestige in today's society.
"Too many people spend money they haven't earned, to buy things they don't want, to impress people they don't like."

In the Old Testament we meet up with King Hezekiah who was a God-fearing man who reigned for twenty-nine years. The name Hezekiah means "Yahweh is my strength" and by following God's directives he accomplished many good things on behalf of his people. However, this one time he slipped up in God's eyes. He was confronted by the prophet Isaiah for his sin. Visitors from Babylon had come to see King Hezekiah and he showed them everything in his palace. He tells Isaiah, "There is nothing among my treasures that I did not show them." He was proud of himself and had forgotten all his wealth was a gift from God.

Isaiah said to Hezekiah, "Hear the word of the Lord of hosts: Behold, the days are coming, when all that is in your house, and that which your fathers have stored up till this day, shall be carried to Babylon. Nothing shall be left, says the Lord (Isaiah 38:5-6).

In the Sermon on the Mount, Jesus intimated there are three basic obstacles to getting to heaven. They are the three selfish P's of power, possessions, and prestige and that is because they feed another pernicious P word called pride. Contrast the three selfish P's and their connection with sin of pride with these key beatitudes contained in Jesus' sermon:

"Blessed are the poor in spirit, for theirs is the kingdom of heaven." "Poor in spirit" means to be humble. Humility is the opposite of pride, the deadliest sin of them all. Pride subsumes power, possessions, and prestige. Thomas Aquinas argued that all sins stem from Pride. "Inordinate self-love is the cause of every sin...the root of pride is found to consist in man not being, in some way, subject to God and His rule."

"Blessed are the meek, for they shall inherit the earth." Jesus was "meek and humble of heart" (Matthew 11:29). He asks us to be obedient to God and rely on God's powerful graces and not on our own self-centered power and control.

"Blessed are the pure of heart, for they shall see God." To be pure of heart means to be free of all selfish intentions and self-seeking desires. St. Thomas asserted, "There is no sin in which, the devil takes so much delight as in impurity; because the flesh is strongly inclined to that vice, and he that falls into it can be rescued from it only with difficulty." Sexual lusters exert their power over others for selfish pleasure.

"Blessed are the peacemakers, for they shall be called children of God." People who live only to acquire personal power, possessions and prestige disturb the peace and tranquility of others. Jesus taught "Peace I leave with you; My peace I give to you" (John 14:27). One cannot give to another what one does not possess in oneself which is peace.

"We serve God by serving others. The world defines greatness in terms of power, possessions, prestige, and position. If you can demand service from others, you've arrived. In our self-serving culture with its me-first mentality, acting like a servant is not a popular concept." – Rick Warren

The Problem of Desiring Power and Prestige in God's
Eyes

"And all the trees of the field shall know
that I, the LORD,
bring low the high tree,
lift high the lowly tree,
wither up the green tree,
and make the withered tree bloom.
As I, the LORD, have spoken, so will I do. Ezekiel 17:24

This passage has a special meaning for the author. For
most of my life I wanted to be a high tree. I sought
prestige. Through God's loving actions in my life, I have
slowly been drawn to becoming a lowly tree. It has been
a long and arduous journey mainly because my great
need to stand out and be recognized has seriously stood
in the way. Often my attempts to lift people up to be
better versions of themselves have not worked because
I relied on power and control instead of support,
encouragement, and respect. God "sets the lowly on
high..." (Job 5:11).

Satan tried to tempt Jesus with power, possessions, and
prestige. After Jesus was in the desert for forty days, he
was obviously very hungry, thirsty, and worn down. His
energy and resistance were at low ebb. Satan tried
three times to entice Jesus to bow down before him,
but Jesus remained obedient to his Father despite all he
was suffering. We could say Jesus became battle-tested
through that very demanding desert experience.

Satan tempts Jesus first with power by having him use
his power to turn stones into bread. He said, "If you are

the Son of God, tell these stones to become bread."
(Matthew 4:3). Jesus refuses Satan and cites scripture
instead. Jesus answered him, "It is written, 'Man must
not live only on bread. He must also live on every word
that comes from the mouth of God.'"

Since the temptation to demonstrate Jesus' power did
not work, Satan tried to tempt him with his prominence
(prestige) as the Son of God. Satan takes Jesus to the
holy city and had him stand on the highest point of the
temple.

"If you are the Son of God," he said, "throw yourself
down. It is written,
'The Lord will command his angels to take good care of
you. They will lift you up in their hands.
Then you won't trip over a stone'" (Psalm 91:11-12)

Jesus answered him, "It is also written, 'Do not test the
Lord your God'" (Deuteronomy 6:16).

Finally, Satan as the prince of the world, tries to tempt
Jesus with possession of the world and all the prestige
which goes along with it. He takes Jesus to a very high
mountain. He shows him all the kingdoms of the world
and their glory and said, "If you bow down and worship
me, I will give you all this." Jesus said to him, "Get away
from me, Satan! It is written, 'Worship the Lord your
God. He is the only one you should serve"
(Deuteronomy 6:13). Then Satan left Jesus and angels
came and took care of him.

Satan uses the same temptations of power, possessions
and prestige on us over and over again. As William

Arthur Ward advises us, "Greatness is not found in possessions, power, position, or prestige. It is discovered in goodness, humility, service, and character." Every time we draw on God's power to fight and overcome Satan's enticements, we develop stronger fortitude in face of the next onslaughts coming out from the dastardly prince of evil's world. "Every conquering temptation represents a new fund of moral energy. Every trial endured and weathered in the right spirit makes a soul nobler and stronger than it was before" (William Butler Yeats).

The Environment of the World

"Lord, guide me to everlasting life!" People die in this world. Everlasting life has to exist some other place than this world. But we are here now in this world environment. Robert Frost wrote about "two roads" in our life. Using that example, there are two guides to two different roads to our final destination. One leads us to everlasting life. The other guide would lead us to believe the world is the end of the line-the final destination. The evil guide does his best not to bring up another destination he knows too well. Both guides say, "follow me!" One guide teaches us to love other people despite their flaws, mistakes, and sinfulness and help them attain everlasting life. The other guide teaches us to reap as much pleasure out of this life as you can because "you only go around once" and then you die.

C. S. Lewis said, "If we find ourselves with a desire that nothing in this world can satisfy, the most probable explanation is that we were made for another world."

Returning to the person-environment fit model, where is the greatest clash or mismatch between the person, if it us, and the environment in the current world? Is it not principally between a person's values and the advertised reinforcers provided by the environment? The advertised and promoted reinforcers are power, possessions, pleasure and prestige. They will lead us to personal satisfaction. But you and I know better. We are being sold a bill of goods. We have a real problem with the "satisfaction" reward the world environment is selling. There is not a good or acceptable fit between us and the present world culture as it is today because we are made for another place where peace, happiness, joy and love for one another and God reigns supreme.

Violence

"Therefore pride is their necklace; they clothe themselves with violence"- Psalm 73:6

We met Ralph earlier and how his envy and wrath led to acts of violence. Violence has been around since the beginning of time. Recall the stories of envy and wrath in the bible when Cain murdered his brother Abel. In Genesis 4:23-24 Lamech boasts to his wives, "...hear my words. I have killed a man for wounding me, a young man for injuring me. If Cain is avenged seven times, then Lamech seventy-seven times." Years later Joseph's brothers plotted out of envy to kill him.

We tend to forget that violence existed even before the world was created. "Michael and his angels fought against the dragon, and the dragon and his angels fought back. But he was not strong enough, and they lost their place in heaven. The great dragon was hurled down—that ancient serpent called the devil, or Satan, who leads the whole world astray. He was hurled to the earth, and his angels with him" (Revelation 12:7-9).

Satan is the prince of the world, who along with his demons, are doing their best to lead the world astray. One of their primary methods is to get us to hate one another rather than love one another as Jesus taught us. Satan loves violence. In his Christmas Day sermon in 1957, which was written while he was in jail, Rev. Martin Luther King Jr. said, "Hate multiplies hate, violence multiplies violence, and toughness multiplies toughness in a descending spiral of destruction."

During World War I in 1914, Sigmund Freud, a neurologist and the founder of psychoanalysis, shared with a colleague this observation: "Primitive, savage and evil impulses of mankind have not vanished in any individual, but continue their existence, although in a repressed state" waiting for "opportunities to display their activity." Where do these primitive, savage and evil impulses come from? They are connected to original sin.

When Adam and Eve were evicted from the beautiful and peaceful Garden of Eden for their sin, they then faced a dangerous world where the animals and the elements were no longer calm and peaceful. Tigers, bears and snakes and the elements now threatened their survival. Rick Hanson among others believe dangers like those led to the development of a negativity bias that we have genetically inherited from our ancestors. Threats to survival led people to becoming psycho-physiologically impacted more by negative things than positive things in their environment leading to a negativity bias. Not only do negative stimuli trigger more neural activity in brain scans, but research also shows negativity is detected more quickly and easily. In studies conducted by psychologist John Cacioppo, participants were shown pictures of either positive, negative, or neutral images. The researchers then observed electrical activity in the brain. Negative images produced a much stronger response in the cerebral cortex than did positive or neutral images. It helps explain why tragedies were more popular than comedies during Greco-Roman times.

They delighted in tragedies because their "heroes fought hopeless battles with fate and died miserably, in wretchedness and despair. They had this liking for tragedy because it seemed to them to set forth, truthfully and understandably, the conditions of life as they found it: that it appeared to them as a reasonable and accurate picture of human existence" (Mutih Skeini, Quora).

Roman citizens loved to watch violence in live action. The 2,100-year-old Roman Colosseum had the capacity to host 50,000 spectators or "fans in the stands" who would watch brutal gladiatorial battles and decide the fate of the loser-yelling "iugula" (kill him) or "missum" to show mercy. Will it be thumps up or thumbs down?

When people think of Shakespeare's many plays, the two most likely to come to mind are the great tragedies Hamlet and Macbeth. Hamlet singlehandedly kills three people. Six people are murdered in Macbeth. The two plays reveal that the desire or drive to have power and revenge leads to murder.

Violence still sells in today's world and plays to our primitive instincts whether in the movies, video games or the news. Superhero-based films have become an incredibly popular and money-making genre. Researchers from Penn State University College of Medicine analyzed 10 superhero-based films sizing up the violent content in them by compiling the specific acts and types of violence portrayed by the movie's antagonists and protagonists. They found superheroes engage in far more violent acts than the super-villain they face. Both the super heroes and the villains participate in fighting, use lethal weapons, destroy property, murder, and use a combination of bullying, intimidation, and torture. The superheroes committed 168 acts of murder while the villains committed 93.

The researchers state after reviewing the study: "Superheroes depicted in film are often viewed by children and adolescents as "the good guy," and therefore may be influenced by their portrayal of risk-taking behaviors and acts of violence." The American Psychological Association takes the position that children who see violence on television or movies might become less sensitive to the pain of others, more fearful of the world around them, and more likely to engage aggressively.

One of the inappropriate behavioral patterns involves the 'Macho' masculine stereotype of aggression in interacting particularly with the opposite sex. The super hero portrayed in today's movies, videos and video games is not like the super heroes of the past according to Dr. Sharon Lamb, counseling and school psychology professor at the University of Massachusetts, Boston. "Today's superhero is too much like an action hero who participates in non-stop violence; he's aggressive, sarcastic and rarely speaks to the virtue of doing good for humanity. When not in superhero costume, these men, like Ironman, exploit women, flaunt bling and convey their manhood with high-powered guns. "The comic book heroes of the past did fight criminals, she said, "but these were heroes boys could look up to and learn from because outside of their costumes, they were real people with real problems and many vulnerabilities."

Eric Madfis, an associate professor of criminal justice at the University of Washington at Tacoma, said unfortunately, "We teach boys and men that the only socially acceptable emotion to have is not to be vulnerable and sensitive, but to be tough and macho and aggressive."

Many of the popular movies rely on fights, killings, special effects and explosions to hold their audiences. Quentin Tarantino's movies feature and depend upon violence. His film Django Unchained received numerous awards and nominations, winning two out of five nominations at the 85th Academy Awards. The Independent, a British online newspaper, said the movie was part of "the new sadism in cinema" and added, "There is something disconcerting about sitting in a crowded cinema as an audience guffaws at the latest garroting or falls about in hysterics as someone is beheaded or has a limb lopped off" (Geoffrey Macnab, January 11, 2013). In Tarantino's two-part Kill Bill films, 102 people wind up dead due to assassinations and revenge.

Some of the best-selling video games feature violence. Call of Duty: Modern Warfare earned over $600 million within its first three days of release. It is a first-person shooter game set in World War II. The computer supports the player during missions from the perspective of the infantry and combined arms groups. The game follows the Red Army as well as British and American Paratroopers. It is a war game where violence can be justified.

The Grand Theft Auto series on the other hand presents violence for violence's sake. The main character can commit a wide variety of crimes and violent acts including the killing of policemen and military personnel. It was condemned in Britain, Germany, and France due to its "extreme violence." In Grand Theft Auto III, players could pay for the services of prostitutes to restore their health, and if they wished, kill them to get some of their money back. The characters in Grand Theft Auto games commit the sins of murder, lust and pride.

The News Can Be Extremely Depressing

Russell Kolts writes, "Sometimes it seems as if anger is all around us. We flip on the nightly news to hear stories of domestic violence, violent crime, feuding celebrities and politicians, road rage, and countless groups angrily protesting nearly everything imaginable" (The Compassionate-Mind Guide to Managing Your Anger). Watch any newscast for the first story and what it is about. Sometimes they will prepare us that it contains violence. That is because they cannot stop from following journalist Eric Pooley's 1989 axiom, "if it bleeds, it leads."

Always start off with the violent-the bloodier, the better. Some national newscasts will end on a positive note with a happy story that usually takes a few minutes. It is if they know better but cannot stop because the violence sells. Mass shooters know they will be a news sensation and finally will be recognized they believe as a person who has been demeaned by other people who deserve pay back for the killer's hurt and pain. "You now know who I am."

Negativity bias is a primary contributor to violence being central in movies, video games and the news which emphasize tragically negative stories of wars, mass shootings and serial killings over positive stories about acts of human kindness and courage. Negativity bias is an attention-grabber we inherited from our ancestors.

Here are some ways how the negativity bias has showed itself in the author's life.

I conducted a series of successful spiritual retreats. At the end of the last retreat, I forgot the tradition of commending the team members by name in front of the group and felt humiliated. It is the first thing that pops in my mind when I think about all the retreats I led.

During a performance evaluation, I was told my performance exceeded expectations. However, the supervisor said I always seemed preoccupied during group meetings. When I got home my wife asked me "How did it your evaluation go today?" All I could think and talk about was his comment about how I came across in meetings. I spent all the time complaining to her that group meetings seem like a great waste of valuable time. "Did he say anything positive about you," she asked? I mumbled, "He said I was otherwise doing fine."

This bias toward the negative leads us to pay much more attention to the bad things that happen, making them seem much more important than they really are. You might be having a great day at work when a coworker or supervisor makes an offhand comment that you find irritating. You then find yourself stewing and brewing over their words for the rest of the workday or beyond.

Our memories, behaviors and attitudes tend to be shaped and are more reactive to negative stimuli like acts of aggression and violence, negative comments and criticism than positive things like praise.

The accent on the negative over the positive by the brain is to help us keep safe can be seen early on in babies and children. Brain studies indicate that around the seventh month, babies begin to experience greater brain responses to negative than positive stimuli. Babies in the environment of the womb are attached by the umbilical cord to receive air, food, water, and whatever else a mother digests.

The defense in the murder trial of Nicklas Cruz maintained that his birth mother's drug and alcohol addiction damaged his brain as the reason for his alleged mental illness leading to the Parkland mass shooting. His fight at school was the trigger event that set him off. The defense worked as he was sentenced to life in prison without parole instead of a death penalty.

Traumatic events occurring in the environment outside the baby can contribute to trauma experiences in the baby's memory. Arguments, domestic abuse, a mother's emotional stress, being unwanted, neglected or abandoned can contribute to trauma experienced in utero. The author recently was involved in a case where a young woman reacted with extended panic attacks when seeing other people vomit. An interview with her father revealed the daughter was a preemie. One time when she was still in utero, her mother vomited violently. Chances are the baby experienced it as a traumatic event that she was reliving repeatedly which can now pursued in treatment for the daughter using EMDR (Eye Movement Desensitization and Reprocessing) for example.

Researchers Jillian Peterson and James Densley (Warner) found the vast majority of mass shooters in their study experienced early childhood trauma and exposure to violence at a young age. The nature of their exposure included parental suicide, physical or sexual abuse, neglect, domestic violence, and/or severe bullying.

Self-Concept and Self-Worth

"Scarcity of self-value cannot be remedied by money, recognition, affection, attention or influence"- Gary Zukav

Self-concept is a cognitive or mental picture we have of ourselves, while self-esteem is a measure of how much value or worth we feel we have as individuals. Self-concept includes our beliefs and opinions about ourselves, while self-esteem is based on how positively or negatively we view ourselves. A person's self-concept helps them define who they think they are and how they fit into the world and whether they feel as though they belong. The author had dreams of being a Big League pitcher scouted by a professional baseball team while he was in college.

A polio virus at age 22 overwhelmed my physical abilities, but its greatest damage was to my self-image. Very soon it became obvious to me that I would never be a Big League pitcher, run sprints in the outfield to prepare for a game, dance with a pretty girl without braces and crutches or run up and down stairs two steps at a time. I had been dealt a devastating blow to my body but more so to my self-image. It did not help when my little cousin saw me for the first time after coming home from the rehabilitation center walking with braces and crutches said, "You walk like Frankenstein!" as I moved one leg at a time rather than using a swing through gait. Her remark still stings a little bit.

My own experience of an attack on my self-concept led me to want to know more about the role self-concept might have in the lives of mass murderers. Columbine shooter Eric Harris lived with a physical anomaly. He had a chest deformity called pectis excavatum meaning the chest bone sinks into the chest. It would explain why he would avoid taking off his shirt in front of people. Recall earlier in his journal: "I have always hated how I looked, I make fun of people who look like me, sometimes without even thinking sometimes just because I want to rip on myself. That's where a lot of my hate grows from. The fact that I have practically no self-esteem, especially concerning girls and looks and such."

Dylan Klebold, Harris' partner in the Columbine shooting, revealed this about himself in his journal. "What's bad — no girls (friends or girlfriends), no other friends except a few, nobody accepting me even though I want to be accepted, me doing badly & being intimidated in any & all sports, me looking weird & acting shy — BIG problem, me getting bad grades..."

Adam Lanza the Newtown school shooter was 6 feet tall but weighed only 112 pounds attributed to anorexia. One wonders how he felt when he looked at himself in the mirror. Robert Hansen murdered at least seventeen women in Alaska. When he was young, he had a stutter and severe acne that left him permanently scarred. Because he believed the attractive girls in school were not interested in him, he grew up hating them and was driven to seek revenge much like Ted Bundy did.

We live in a society that prizes physical beauty. You can look at the number of ads in the media that hawk beauty products and body-building programs and equipment. It is easy to recognize the effects of idolatry of physique. There is bulimia, anorexia, steroid use, Botox treatments, cosmetic surgery for everything … face lifts, tummy tucks, breast implants, hair transplants, erectile dysfunction remedies and so on.

When we encounter someone whose physical appearance deviates from so called normalcy, like Robert Hansen's acne scars, we can experience aesthetic anxiety which we want to escape from or avoid. We can instantly look the other way from the abnormality to reduce its power as a stimulus. Or, the anxiety can cause "foot-in-the mouth disease" comments, for example, blurting out "I see what you mean" to a blind person resulting in immediate personal embarrassment. Or, talking louder to a person who happens to be in a wheelchair. The latter incident now compounds aesthetic anxiety with the "spread effect".

The spread effect occurs when one deviation from normalcy is spread to the person's whole being. It becomes further exemplified when the person also talks much slower to the person in the wheelchair. Now the person in a wheelchair is seen as not only deaf but obviously slow-witted as well. These shock reactions happen because we live in a society that is in love with a beautiful or "normal" physical body. In Robert Hansen's case his stuttering would be "spread" to a "he's not very smart" deduction.

One's body image among other things can lead to negative self-talk which is self-demeaning.

Mass shootings are most often motivated by revenge or envy. That is why many take place at a school or a workplace where shooters feel rejected, according to Tony Farrenkopf, a forensic psychologist, who has created psychological profiles of mass shooters. "School shooters often harbor anger and paranoid delusions, have low self-esteem and hang out with an outcast group," Farrenkopf said. And there is usually a triggering event — either a lost job or a falling out with a girlfriend — that finally makes them snap, he added. (10 Surprising Facts About the Teen Brain).

Overwhelmingly, mass shooters are men or juvenile boys. Peter Langman, is a psychologist who also has studied mass shooters, offered his perspective. Our culture and media (such as violent movies and video games) only reinforce the notion that manhood is about attaining power, and social and sexual status. Violence is glorified as a way to get that power, he said. Langman noted in the Journal of Campus Behavioral Intervention that "the sense of damaged masculinity is common to many shooters and often involves failures and inadequacies."

Here are some examples of damaged masculinity as the possible motives for two of the most notorious serial killers-Ted Bundy and John Wayne Gacy.

John Wayne Gacy raped, tortured, and murdered at least 33 young men and boys. Environmental threats to his masculinity included (from sources listed in Wikipedia):

• His father belittled him, calling him "dumb and stupid" and compared him unfavorably with his sisters.

• His mother tried to shield him from his father's abuse, which only resulted in accusations that he was a "sissy" and a "mama's boy" who would "probably grow up queer."

• When he was around 7 years of age, a family friend and contractor would sometimes molest Gacy in his truck.

• He was overweight and unathletic as a child.

Gacy claimed he still loved his father, but felt he was "never good enough" in his father's eyes.

Ted Bundy kidnapped, raped, and murdered at least 30 young women and girls. He was born out of wedlock and raised by grandparents. His grandfather Samuel was described as a tyrannical bully who beat his wife and dog in the front of young Ted. After Bundy was incarcerated, he told an interviewer that he "identified with," "respected," and "clung to" his grandfather.

His self-image as a masculine male could have been threatened by several reported facts about him:

• Early on, he dealt with a speech impediment.

• He was not athletic.

• The first girl he dated rejected him describing him as "pitifully weak" (Antonia Paget, Mirror, December 18, 2019).

Her rejection of him could definitely help explain Bundy's maniacal revenge by hunting for young white college students with brown hair parted down the middle who looked like the young woman who dumped him. And did he model his grandfather's behavior of violence as the person he "identified with?"

Hans Toch, a social psychologist and criminologist, interviewed sixty-nine prison inmates and parolees who had a history of violence. He found the most common characteristic involves aggression in defense of self-image or to promote self-image. Aggressive feats become a matter of pride from which the person could derive a sense of self-worth in reaction to feelings of low self-esteem. (H. Toch, Violent Men).

The negative things people tell us about our self during childhood can become incorporated into our self-concept as truths about us. What they say about us can become what we say to ourself called negative self-talk. We can imagine Gacy telling himself "I'm a sissy" or Klebold telling himself "I'm weird looking!" Negative self-talk can be self-destructive.

Negative Self-Talk

Self-statements can be positive or negative. Negative self-statements can cause mental, physical and spiritual damage to oneself. Studies show that when people engage in negative self-talk, they are more likely to suffer from anxiety, depression, and low self-esteem. It also can lead to social isolation and loneliness because most people do not enjoy being around negative people.

Here are a couple of examples of negative self-talk: "I'm dumb" and "There's no use" are statements that stem from thoughts and emotions. I always feel sad when I hear someone say things like that in front of me. I'm sadder when it comes from a child and deeply pained if it came from one of my own children. "I'm dumb" is a direct assault on one's self-esteem and self-concept. "There's no use" means a lack of motivation and self-defeat. There are many more examples of negative self-talk. You might be on the lookout for those you might say to yourself and catch them, then nail the underlying thoughts and emotions.

Find out where they come from. In what situations are negative self-put downs more apt to raise up? In short, recognize them for what they are and put a plan in action to catch them before it happens. Negative self-talk is self-sabotage. What's worse, it can develop into a curse which can cause even greater self-damage. They can lead to a self-fulfilling prophecy. What you say can happen to you.

"Death and life are in the power of the tongue, and those who love it will eat its fruits."
A popular take-off on this invaluable piece of wisdom is "Words kill, words give life. They are either poison or fruit. You choose."
This means even seemingly idle words that come out of our mouths can have impact on our principal judgment at death. This belief receives strong support from the following scriptural passage: "I tell you, on the day of judgment men will render account for every careless word they utter" (Matthew 12:36).

I immediately thought of all the seemingly careless and off-the-cuff hurtful remarks I have spoken to myself and others. They were not fully erased from my memory but stared me right in my face as judgments against me. Talk about a scary examination of conscience! Whether I meant it or not does not make any difference.

I recall those times in counseling when a person remembered their mother saying to them as a child, "I wish you were never born" or "Why can't you do anything right!" I instantly felt their pain and how that one statement can possibly curse the person for the rest of their life. I also remember a good friend confessing to me one morning over a cup of coffee that when he was a little boy his father told him to go in the garage and get a wrench for him while he was fixing a broken bicycle. When little Jimmy happily returned with some pliers instead of the wrench his father yelled at him, "You are as useless as tits on a bull." He shared this one incident that occurred over forty years ago with tears in his eyes. He added that he gets nervous to this day whenever he is faced with doing anything that smacks of using tools or is mechanical in nature.

The first thing that I immediately thought about after listening to my friend and comforting him was to search for those nasty and hurtful things I could remember saying to my wife and my children. One never knows which off-handed remarks can have a residual hurtful effect.

We have learned that school shooters write negative self-statements about their physical appearance and poor social life in their journals. Research has found that children who engage in negative self-talk at an early age are more likely to experience negative moods, depression and act aggressively toward others, and are higher risks for suicide.

The reader might want to examine their own tendencies with their tongue. The other day I caught myself saying, "That was certainly a dumb thing to do." I could have said, "You sure are a dumb-head, you are always forgetting things!" Could I be cursing myself with second statement? I am not one who sees Satan in every cornflake, but I sure do worry that I might not be taking this self-cursing seriously enough. Here are some statements as examples. See which ones lead you to wince or that you would never want to say to yourself.

"I'm tired of living"
"Nothing ever goes right.... What's the use, I give up!"
"I just can't take it anymore"

"It runs in the family, so it's just a matter of time before
it happens to me"
"I'm sick and tired of being sick and tired"
"I'm just a clumsy kind of person"
"Here I go ahead making bad decisions"

This should bring to mind that what we say with our
tongue can possibly grow into a self-imposed curse. It
confirms for me the frightening power of our words.

My wife Pat asked me one time if I could find a green
boomerang on the Internet that our little five-year-old
granddaughter had asked for. It suddenly became clear
to me that unkind and harmful words can act just like a
boomerang. What you cast out of your mouth can come
back and strike you back particularly if you are not
paying attention to what negative things you have said
about yourself to yourself. Sticks and stones can break
your bones and so can words in the form of negative
self-talk cause damage to us as well.

Negativity has its own spread effect when criticism of
others acts like a boomerang.

The Negativity of Criticism

"Do not rejoice when your enemy falls,

and let not your heart be glad when he stumbles"

Proverbs 24:17

Criticism is like a boomerang or maybe more like a seesaw because when we are putting another person down, we are indirectly boosting our own fragile ego up. Criticism is a psychological defense mechanism that functions to protect a person from anxiety-producing thoughts and feelings. Temporarily it makes you feel better about yourself, but then you realize in time it is only leading you to feeling worse about yourself for being so judgmental and critical. We live in a judgmental society. In our society it is tough being on the receiving end of criticism worrying and fearing about how people "Think of us." Deep down, even the most critical person is yearning for the acceptance they most likely deny to others.

Learning about or watching other people making mistakes, even little ones, can make us feel good about ourselves. You might blame it on the negativity bias built into us.

"A misdeed will ruin a hero's reputation more than a good deed will improve a villain's – Rick Hanson

Bill Buckner was an All-Star and baseball batting champion. He helped the Dodgers win the pennant with a .314 batting average in 1974. He won the National League batting title with a .324 mark in 1980 with the

Chicago Cubs. He was named to the All-Star team in 1981 as he led the major leagues in doubles. After setting a major league record for first basemen with 159 assists in 1982, Buckner surpassed that total with 161 in 1983 while again leading the NL in doubles. All these "positives" about Bill Buckner's accomplishments as a professional Big League player tarnished his record by one fatal mistake as a fielder on the baseball diamond called an "error."

One ground ball coming his way changed his legacy forever. He made one of the biggest blunders in baseball history when he let Mookie Wilson's easy roller through his Boston Red Sox legs during the 1986 World Series. It led to years of fan anger and public mockery of him. Indeed, one misplay led to ruining his reputation.

Steve Bartman, a fan in the stands at Wrigley Field, was soon to be hated by his fellow fans for causing their team he was rooting for to lose a critical game. His great mistake occurred during a playoff baseball game on October 14, 2003, when several spectators, including Steve Bartman, attempted to catch a foul ball in Game 6 of the National League Championship Series between the Chicago Cubs and the Florida Marlins. Cubs outfielder Moisés Alou claimed Bartman reached out for the ball and prevented him from catching the ball for an out.

It was seen as a turning point in the series because the Cubs were only five outs away from clinching the National League pennant. "In the moments following the play, Cubs fans shouted insults and threw debris at Bartman. For his safety, security was forced to escort him from the ballpark. Minutes after the game, his name and personal information were published online, necessitating police protection at his home" (Wikipedia). The Cubs could have overcome the loss of the one out but did not. Pitcher Mark Prior threw a costly wild pitch and shortstop Alex Gonzalez mishandled a ground ball that could have resulted in an inning-ending double play. These mistakes ultimately led to eight runs in the one inning, and the Cubs lost the game 8–3. They had another opportunity to win the series in Game 7 at their home park the next day, but they were eliminated by the Marlins.

All Bartman did was to reach out for a ball heading toward the stands for a souvenir and happy memory like any brave and enthusiastic fan does. Most people who first met him would not see him in a negative light, but once he made that grave mistake, he deserved to be hated for it in their minds.

Many absolutely worst mistakes have happened without knowing the person to blame for it. For example, the Titanic's lookouts had no binoculars.

What about the Trojan Horse? The horse was taken in through the gates while Troy slept. The Greek warriors emerged from this hollow horse, and opened up the gates of Troy, which allowed the Greek army to enter and ultimately led to the fall of the once impenetrable city of Troy. Who is the person that welcomed the Trojan Horse through the gates? We have to have someone to blame for it.

Eric Harris criticized not only the students in his school but all the humans in the world for being stupid. He had an undying hatred of the human race and wrote about his desire for its total annihilation. He "would get rid of all the fat, retarded, crippled, stupid, dumb, ignorant, worthless people of this world. No one is worthy of this planet, only me and who ever I choose...Everyone should be shot out into space and only those people I say should be left behind."

When a person puts other people down, they are trying to build a fragile ego up. Harris knew what he was doing. "It's ok if I am a hypocrite, but no one else, because I am higher than you people, no matter what you say if you disagree, I would shoot you."

When we examine the motives of mass shooters and serial killers certain ones of the seven capital or deadly sins rise to the top. They are principally Pride, Lust, Wrath and Envy. Greed, Gluttony and Sloth are more in the background.

We need not forget the interconnection with power, possessions, pleasure and prestige. Pride, Wrath and especially Lust would appear to be dominant motives in the lives of serial killers like Dahmer, Bundy, Hansen, Ridgeway and Gacy. Pride, Envy and Wrath dominated Harris and Klebold, Cruz, Ramos and Jouett to punish students and the school environment for their academic and social lives.

The Seven Deadly Sins

Pursuit of power, possessions, prestige and pleasure is not sinful in its own right but it is about how much a person values them and goes about obtaining them. The number "seven" in the number of cardinal, capital or deadly sins has biblical prominence as it appears 518 times in the New International Version of the Bible. For example, God created the world in six days and rested on the seventh day after his work was completed. The Book of Revelation is filled with many sevens including 7 churches, 7 bowls, 7 angels, 7 trumpets, 7 seals, etc. Seven's connection to sin appears in reference to Mary Magdalene. "...and also, some women who had been cured of evil spirits and diseases: Mary (called Magdalene) from whom seven demons had come out" (Luke 8:2). And further about demons, "Then it goes and takes seven other spirits more wicked than itself, and they go in and live there. And the final condition of that person is worse than the first."

Seven is connected to the forgiveness of sins. Peter asked Jesus, "Lord, how many times shall I forgive my brother or sister who sins against me? Up to seven times?" Jesus answered, "I tell you, not seven times, but seventy-seven times" (Matthew 18:21-22).

I am not sure why the early Christian church decided there would be seven instead of six or eight capital or deadly sins, but it is consistent with the meaning of seven in the bible. Seven means completeness or fullness. The list of the Seven Deadly Sins can be considered a full and complete list.

Pope Gregory I ("the Great") in 590 A.D. codified the list of seven deadly sins of lust, gluttony, sloth, greed, envy, wrath, and pride.

When we examine the motives of mass shooters and serial killers certain ones of the seven capital or deadly sins rise to the top. They are principally Pride, Lust, Wrath and Envy. Greed, Gluttony and Sloth are of secondary importance.

Scientists have explored the sins of killers. Herrero, et al, questioned and analyzed 30 serial killers from America and Europe in order to determine the major sins behind their decisions to commit crimes. The results show a predominance of pride, lust and greed as the main motivators within the study sample.

Sins of violence, hatred, racism, abortion, mass murders, suicides, drug abuse, religious persecutions, rampant child sexual abuse and sex trafficking abound in America and throughout the world. For mass murderers and serial killers, the strongest underlying and unifying deadly sin is pride. Killers on this scale use their power of violence to make them feel important and they hope notorious. Dennis Rader played with the police and the news media to show how smart and clever he was. School shooters attempt to outdo their predecessors to attain an even bigger name in the media. Cruz bragged, "And when you see me on the news, you'll all know who I am."

Fame-seeking shooters like Cruz and others are more likely to receive media coverage than their lesser counterparts according to a research report by Silva and Greene-Colozzizi titled "Fame-seeking mass shooters in America: Severity, characteristics, and media coverage."

Notoriety, fame, name recognition, popularity and prestige can lead to the sin of Pride which is the overriding basis for all the seven deadly sins.

Pride, the Root of All Sin and All Evil

"Therefore pride is their necklace; they clothe themselves with violence"- Psalm 73:6

Thomas Aquinas argued that all other sins stem from Pride, making this one of the most important sins to focus on: "Inordinate self-love is the cause of every sin...the root of pride is found to consist in man not being, in some way, subject to God and His rule." Pope Gregory the Great called the sin of pride the "queen of them all." In Dante's "Purgatorio," the second part of his Divine Comedy, pride is at the bottom of Mount Purgatory as the deepest and deadliest sin. The penitent's punishment for the sin of pride is to carry such heavy weights that their heads are bent down, rendering them unable to challenge anyone with their defiant eyes. If a person is beleaguered by the sin of Pride, they will now know what they can expect to face if they do not change their ways.

The opposite of pride is humility. "Humility is not thinking less of yourself, it's thinking of yourself less" says Rick Warren. "Humility, (is) that low, sweet root, from which all heavenly virtues shoot" (Thomas More).

We need to be more like little children. "To become a child in relation to God is the condition for entering the kingdom. For this, we must humble ourselves and become little" (CCC 526). Little children have not yet learned what pride is. A young child trusts with all his heart that his parents will be there for him in his time of need. A child trusts that his father or mother will be there for him when he takes those first steps, or when she takes her first ride on a new tricycle. A child trusts that his mom or dad will be there for him when he scrapes his knee, or when the other kids are picking on him. We who wish to enter heaven must too, manifest a humble, loving trust in God.

St. Augustine who lived a life of sin in his earlier years shared about his change in heart, "Proud as I was, I dared to seek that which only the humble can find."

If we want the devil to leave us alone, we need to humble ourselves as James proclaimed: "Submit therefore to God. Resist the devil and he will flee from you" (James 4:7). This little tidbit illustrates how humility works in action: Satan appeared to a little monk, assuming the appearance of a holy angel, and said to him, "I am the angel Gabriel and I am sent unto thee." But the monk said, "Consider well if you were not in fact sent to some other: for I am not worthy that an angel should be sent to me." And Satan quickly departed with a flourish.

Envy

Ted Bundy envied the men the woman who rejected him found to her liking. Eric Harris envied the guys the Columbine school girls found attractive. "I have practically no self-esteem, especially concerning girls…"

While pride is the basis for all the Seven Deadly Sins, envy is the most counterproductive sin because it provides no sense of real pleasure or the least bit of personal happiness. Joseph Epstein said, "Of the seven deadly sins, only envy is no fun at all." Eric Harris and Dylan Klebold and others likely understood and accepted that envy does not help you feel better about yourself. In Dante's "Purgatory," the envious are punished by having their eyes sewn shut with wire.

Bottled up in envy is a sense of resentment. "They have what I want." It can be a house, a car, their happiness, success, the job, their wife or husband, their money, their luck, their looks, their social circle, their way with words, ability to travel whenever and wherever they want, how many friends they have, so for and so on. For school shooters like Harris and Klebold, they envied other students for their looks, social life, girl appeal, grades and athletic abilities.

Envy is a sick, sneaky, and sadistic sin. How does envy show itself in one's life?

- By gossiping or spreading rumors

- Talking behind people's back

• Feeling upset by other people's good fortune

• By spying on or stalking others

• Bullying others

• Verbally abusing other people

• By physically hurting other people

At this point, chances the reader might be feeling you do not have any issues with envy.

• Do you ever feel bad when a friend gets more birthday or anniversary wishes than you do on Facebook?

• Do you ever feel "personally pained" when you learn of a friend's achievement that you wish you had or could attain?

• When you are not invited to a party that your other friends are attending, what is the feeling you have inside? Envy, anger, resentment, or depression? Do you ask yourself, "What is it about me?"
In short, to feel envious, three conditions need to be met:

1.   A person or people have something you want
2.   You don't have what they've got
3.   You feel personally pained because they have it
        and you do not. There is a general or specific
        feeling of underlying unfairness about it.

Envy has plagued mortals from the beginning of time. Adam and Eve envied something God possessed symbolized by the forbidden "Tree of Knowledge" that led them to committing the original sin. Even before their time, Satan demonstrated his envy and hatred toward God's supremacy over the angels he had created. Subservience led to Satan's viewpoint in Milton's Paradise Lost, "Better to reign in hell than to serve in Heaven" (1.263). To "serve" in Heaven was degrading for him so he would become a "king" with his "princes" in hell. Satan convinced himself and his fellow fallen angels that they will be freer and happier in Hell.

Cain and Abel

The Lord looked with favor on Abel and his offering, but on Cain and his offering he did not look with favor. So, Cain was very angry and dejected" (Genesis 4:3-5). Cain became so envious of Abel he killed him.

Joseph and his brothers

Joseph was the favorite of all of Jacob's sons and made him "a long-ornamented tunic" described in modern times as Joseph's "amazing technicolor coat". Joseph shared his dreams with his father and brothers that suggested that he was special, and they should bow down before him. "When his brothers saw that their father loved him best, they hated him so much that they could not say a kind word to him" (37:4).

One day, his father sent Joseph out to check on his brothers who were attending the flocks. When his brothers saw him coming, they plotted, out of envy, to kill him. "They said to one another: "Here comes that dreamer! Come now, let us kill him and throw him into one of the cisterns here; we could say that a wild beast devoured him" (37:20).

There are many more stories of envy in the Old Testament. Jacob and his mother Rebekah envied Esau's birthright and plotted how to steal the father's forthcoming blessing from Esau. Later, Jacob becomes involved with the two daughters of Laban named Rachel and Leah. Jacob loved Rachel but due to trickery by their father Laban, Jacob slept with Leah instead of Rachel on the wedding night. Leah envied her beautiful sister Rachel and could not get Jacob to love her even though she bore him children.

With time King Saul saw David no longer as a friend and upper comer, but now as a competitor, and became deeply envious of him and wanted him dead.

David had Bathsheba's husband killed out of envy.

The Story of the Prodigal Son is about two brothers and their father. The older brother is out in the field when he hears the sounds of celebration. He is envious and angry to find his father has killed the fatted calf for this ungrateful younger brother who has returned home after wasting all the money the father gave him. His father never held such a celebration for him. But they must celebrate because the father thought his son was dead but is now alive. The father reassures his unhappy older son that everything he has is his. In the older son's eyes, it still doesn't seem fair.

The Sadducees and Pharisees Envied Jesus

The New Testament makes it clear that the chief scribes envied and hated Jesus when they "saw the wonderful things he did and the children shouting in the temple courts, "Hosanna to the Son of David" (Matthew 21:25). Mark claimed, "...for they feared him, because the whole crowd was amazed at his teaching" (Mark 11:18). In time it led the chief priests and the elders of the people assembled in the palace of the high priest, whose name was Caiaphas, to decide to kill Jesus.

In today's world envy happens in the workplace.

Mary Ann received a special award for her excellence in nursing care. The hospital administrator announced her award at a staff meeting and she was honored during a special afternoon reception. She had been a nurse for more than 20 years, and this was the first time she was recognized by the hospital. She was thrilled with the award.

In the next few weeks, she noticed that her assignments were becoming more demanding than usual to the point she was becoming absolutely worn out before the shift ended. She couldn't stop for a minute and noticed the other nurses were sitting at the desk and chatting. In time, a friend of hers took her aside and told her she overheard a conversation between the nurse-in-charge and another nurse about a new patient transfer who required special attention. She said in a sarcastic tone, "I'm going to give him to Mary Ann our "star nurse" on the floor because she's so special."

Facebook Envy

Several researchers have described what they call
"Facebook envy." College students in one study stated
in response to postings from their friend's feelings of
envy and depression:
"I wish I could travel as much as some of my friends do."
"Many of my friends have a better life than me. I wish I
could be like them."
"Many of my friends are happier than me."

Ethan Kross, professor of psychology at the University
of Michigan who studies the impact of Facebook on our
wellbeing claimed, "Envy is being taken to an extreme."
We are constantly bombarded by "Photoshopped lives,"
he says, "and that exerts a toll on us the likes of which
we have never experienced in the history of our species.
And it is not particularly pleasant."

Fake Fronts and False Faces

I was telling a visiting nurse I was writing about envy
and asked her how and when she sees envy showing up
as she is an avid Facebook user. She surprised me by
saying that several of her friends put a false face
forward belying the sad truth in their lives. They brag
about how happy they are when she knows their
marriages are on the rocks or they post an updated
selfie suggesting "life is great" when she knows they are
suffering with deep depression. She said, "They are
faking it by appearing to be happy when inside they are
envious of the lives of other people, they know
including mine." Envy is a desire for what one doesn't

have with the root often being low self-esteem. It is a cover-up of the true feelings of sadness with one's life. "Envy, though not the greatest sin, is the only one that gives the sinner no pleasure at all, not even fake and temporary satisfaction"- Peter Kreeft.

Lust

Lust was found to be the second major sin committed by the 30 serial killers in the study presented earlier. Lust is a nasty sin. For most serial killers like Bundy, Dahmer, Hansen and Gacy they feasted on sexual pleasure. St. Bernard and St. Isidore said, "The human race is brought under the power of the devil more by lust than by all the other vices." Wikipedia says this about lust. "Lust, or lechery is intense longing. It is usually thought of as intense or unbridled sexual desire, which may lead to fornication, adultery, rape, bestiality and other sinful sexual acts". They did not include murder.

The people in Sodom and Gomorrah and the surrounding towns "gave themselves up to sexual immorality and perversion. They serve as an example of those who suffer the punishment of eternal fire" (Jude 1:7). They were killed for their sins.

People living in today's world seem clueless to the destructive effects the sin of lust has on families, women, on children and society at large.

"Of all the worldly passions, lust is the most intense. All other worldly passions seem to follow in its train."- Buddha

The Eyes

In Dante's Purgatorio, the envious had their eyes sewn shut as their punishment. It seems like an appropriate punishment for lusters as well. Dante's punishment for the lustful is to be whipped around in hurricane-like winds for all eternity.

Shakespeare said, "The eyes are the window to your soul." In the New Testament, Matthew pictures the eye as the "lamp of the body" and adds "If your eyes are healthy, your whole body will be full of light. But if your eyes are unhealthy, your whole body will be full of darkness. If then the light within you is darkness, how great is that darkness!" (Matthew 6:22-23). A third way of understanding the purpose of our eyes metaphorically is they are the "doorway to our mind".

Job understood the connection between the eyes and sin. "I made a covenant with my eyes not to look lustfully at a young woman" (Job 31:1). Jesus said, "But I tell you that anyone who looks at a woman lustfully has already committed adultery with her in his heart" (Matthew 5:28).

As eyes are the doorway to the mind they can lead to sinful thoughts and actions. One of the main keys to protecting the mind from temptation is control of the eyes. The eyes can lead an individual to any of the seven deadly sins and most certainly to sin of Lust. When a person is consumed with lust or any other sin originating through the eyes, Jesus provided this severe remedy. "If your right eye makes you stumble, tear it out and throw it from you; for it is better for you to lose one of the parts of your body, than for your whole body to be thrown into hell" (Matthew 5:29).

There is no better example of the consequences from the twin sins of pride and lust than in Adam and Eve's case. Genesis 6:6: "When the woman saw that the fruit of the tree was good for food and pleasing to the eye, and also desirable for gaining wisdom, she took some and ate it. She also gave some to her husband, who was with her, and he ate it." It was "pleasing to the eye" sets into motion lust for the forbidden fruit of knowledge.

The lust of the flesh = I want it.

The lust of the eyes = It is so pretty.

The pride of life = It will make me intelligent like God.

Pride and lust result from selfishness. They have always been Satan's most effective tools to use with people. When Eve sinned in the Garden, she believed that if she would eat the forbidden fruit, she would "be like God"- knowing good and evil" (Genesis 3:16). "Then the eyes of both of them were opened, and they realized they were naked; so, they sewed fig leaves together and made coverings for themselves" (Genesis 3:7). They not only hid from God, but they also covered their nakedness with fig leaf as loincloths to cover their genitals.

Eyes played a dramatic part in two other Bible stories.

King David

"One evening David got up from his bed and walked around on the roof of the palace. From the roof he saw a woman bathing. The woman was unbelievably beautiful, and David sent someone to find out about her. The man said, "She is Bathsheba, the daughter of Eliam and the wife of Uriah the Hittite." Then David sent messengers to get her. She came to him, and he slept with her. Then she went back home. The woman conceived and sent word to David, saying, "I am pregnant" (2 Samuel 2:5).
We learn "King David allowed his lust for a woman to lead him to adultery. His cover-up tactics didn't work, so he killed her innocent husband" (2 Samuel 11).

David's lust led to grave consequences.
"But because by doing this you have made the enemies of the Lord show utter contempt, the son born to you will die" (2 Samuel 12:14). Amnon, David's firstborn, raped his half-sister Tamar and was then killed by Absalom her brother. David's son Solomon could not control his lust. Solomon had 700 wives and 300 concubines including many foreigners which angered God. "When Solomon was old, his wives turned his heart away to follow other gods; and his heart was not wholly devoted to the LORD his God, as the heart of his father David had been. (1 Kings 11:4).

David later repented of this sin, but the effect of his sins spread to his children who imitated his lustfulness. As a punishment, God sent a plague upon Israel. "Seventy thousand men" died as a result.
Lust involves a choice and an act of the will. King David chose to give into the temptation to sleep with Bathsheba knowing she was a married woman. He then

has her husband murdered so he could have her all to himself. The great King David committed adultery and then murder in response to lusting for Bathsheba after he sees her bathing.

A story in the Book of Daniel (Catholic Bible) this time has two men seeing a beautiful woman bathing in a garden. She was the wife of Joakim. Her name was Susanna.

"Once, while two elders were watching for an opportune day, she went in as before with only two maids, and wished to bathe in the garden, for it was a hot day. No one was there except the two elders, who had hidden themselves and were watching her. She said to her maids, "Bring me olive oil and ointments, and shut the garden doors so that I can bathe." They did as she told them: they shut the doors of the garden and went out by the side doors to bring what they had been commanded; they did not see the elders, because they were hiding.
When the maids had gone out, the two elders got up and ran to her. They said, "Look, the garden doors are shut, and no one can see us. We are burning with desire for you; so, give your consent, and lie with us. If you refuse, we will testify against you that a young man was with you, and this was why you sent your maids away."

She refuses them so they came to see Joakim the next day claiming they saw a young man, who was hiding, come to her and lay with her. They stated as an adulteress she must be put to death. Because they were elders of the people and judges, the assembly believed them and condemned her to death.

Susanna cried out to God in her innocence. God hears her plea and prompts the prophet Daniel to come to her aid. He uses the tactic of separating the two witnesses. He asks the first elder, "Now then, if you really saw this woman, tell me this: Under what tree did you see them being intimate with each other?" He answered, "Under a mastic tree." He asks the second elder the same question. He answered, "Under an evergreen oak."

Daniel said to each of them, "Very well! This lie has cost you also your head, for the angel of God is waiting with his sword to split you in two, so as to destroy you both. "Following the law of Moses, the lying elders were put to death. "Thus, innocent blood was spared that day."

"Look but don't touch" is a familiar phrase to most people. Knowing the relationship of the eyes to lust, oglers, voyeurs, and viewers in general are cautioned if looking leads to lustful thoughts, you better stop looking. If you do not, it likely will lead to giving into the sins of the flesh. The cultural idea of, "It's okay to look if you don't touch" is not the teaching of Jesus. As we are reminded in 1 John 2:15-16: "Love not the world, neither the things that are in the world. If any man loves the world, the love of the Father is not in him. For all that is in the world, the lust of the flesh, and the lust of the eyes, and the pride of life, is not of the Father, but is of the world."

The twin sins of lust and pride are rampant in our world today due to a selfish need to obtain sexual pleasure wherever possible by using immoral means. It results in abortion, rape, adultery, divorce, child sexual abuse, destruction of families and a plague of pornography.

Most tragically, lust and pride led Ted Bundy, John
Wayne Gacy, Dennis Rader and Richard Hansen among
others to many murders.

The Other Deadly Sins

Gluttony as a sinful nature has expanded in its manifestations. The immediate association is excessive eating and drinking to the point of endangering one's health and well-being. There is a darkly humorous scene in Monty Python's movie The Meaning of Life. A very overweight diner has absolutely stuffed himself and knows he cannot consume anything more. The waiter decides to tempt him with more. He pressures him into eating just a tiny thin after-dinner mint. After a series of refusals, the diner accepts only to have his body explode apart in the restaurant in a sickly mess. The gluttons in *Purgatorio* experience excruciating hunger and thirst while there are plenty of trees with fruit around them. The souls experience this because they can never reach the trees.

There are other opportunities for gluttonous behavior than over-consumption of food or drink. Alcohol and drug addiction are rampant in our society. The Centers for Disease Control and Prevention (CDC) reported 105,000 drug overdose cases contributed to an unprecedented decline in U.S. life expectancy in 2021.

Today we are seeing an overindulgence of porn and video games. Taiwan news reported that a "Man dies after a 3-day Internet gaming binge." He was the second person in Taiwan in 2015 to die while playing online games allegedly due to over-consumption. A seventeen-year-old in Russia died from 22 straight days of playing video games. Cause of death: a thrombosis that occurs when someone stays still for a long period of time without moving around to keep blood flowing.

This gaming addiction phenomenon spawned a new book called Death by Video Game by Simon Parkin. Just as a person can die from overindulgence of video games, they can spiritually die from too much porn. It is easy to see the connection between gluttony and lust in the case of a porn obsession.

Greed

Greed was the third major sin resulting from the study of serial killers. Greed is really an underlying obsession with power. Greedy people seek more power over the people around them principally with money as the measurement stick. It is easily linked with Pride if the primary motivation is to gain respect and prestige. "Look at my big house, my fancy automobile, what does that tell you about me?" asks the braggart. Greed is wrong when we love created things more than God or our neighbor. The punishment for greed in Purgatorio is to lie on the floor, face down, with their hands and feet bound together for desiring material goods with extravagance, greed, or ambition.

Wrath consists of uncontrolled feelings of anger, rage, or hatred. It usually involves extreme anger, spite, resentment, and vengeance. Cain's envy of Abel led to his wrath.

Another example is the famous prolonged history of the Hatfields and the McCoys. In Dante's Purgatorio those with wrathful dispositions are forced to walk through thick acrid smoke that is darker than night. That would dampen a fiery disposition inside the soul.

"In your anger do not sin: Do not let the sun go down while you
are still angry and do not have your anger lead to sinful wrath"
- Ephesians 4:26

Sloth can be equated with physical laziness. Sloth as a sin is not centered on physical activity but rather spiritual laziness and apathy. Thinking about God fades into the background of our lives as we pay more attention to what the world dangles in front of us. It is turning away from moral obligations and toward selfish pursuits. In the process, we lose our spiritual fitness and become more open to temptation and sin. Sloth can occur when a person anticipates failure of their actions to reach success. So why try in the first place. Slothful penitents in *Purgatorio* must shout examples of zeal and show that their punishment is to run without rest.

We end with a mass murderer who allegedly committed all seven deadly sins in his life and bragged about it. In 2014, Elliot Rodger killed six people and injured fourteen others and published beforehand an autobiography titled "My Twisted World", detailing his life starting from his birth. Dorothy Cummings McLean's article "The Isla Vista Killer and the Seven Deadly Sins" (The Catholic World Report) ties Rodger's life history of events to each and every one of the seven deadly sins.

Because this book centers on the sins of pride, envy and lust, Rodgers's connections to these three sins is taken from the article.

For pride, he describes himself as "an intellectual" who would not demean himself by accepting a low-status job. The writer states, "He is outraged that girls do not see how desirable he is..."

She notes, "Above all, envy" dominates his mind and emotions. "He drops out of classes when he discovers his prettiest classmates have boyfriends" and girls do not find him attractive.

His envy becomes intricately connected to a burgeoning interest in lust when he is introduced to pictures of naked women at age 11 and then develops an attachment to porn. Rodgers wrote, "Finding out about sex is one of the things that truly destroyed my entire life." His inability to have sex with a woman, when other young men had no trouble, led to his wrath and raging directed at "humanity" and especially toward women.

Satan

What is Satan's stake in the seven deadly sins? Satan and his demons rely on dangling the temptations of power, possessions, pleasure and prestige as bait to lead people to sin.

Satan used them with Jesus in the desert without success. But they worked well in his first meeting with humans in the Garden of Eden. He continues to use them in the on-going war to win over as many human souls as possible using guerrilla tactics. One tactic is to create the doubt in many people's minds he even exists.

Pope Francis said during a Mass right before Halloween, "This generation, and many others, have been led to believe that the devil is a myth, a figure, an idea, the idea of evil. But the devil exists and we must fight against him." The Devil is a real person, "armed with dark powers," he declared in a television interview in December 2017.

The most renowned exorcist in Rome was the late Father Gabriele Amorth. He claimed, "Remember when we jeer at the devil and tell ourselves he does not exist, that is when he is the happiest."

The poet Charles Baudelaire is credited with saying, "The Devil's cleverest wile is to convince us that he does not exist."

In his book Life of Christ, Archbishop Fulton Sheen, wrote, "Very few people believe in the devil these days, which suits the devil very well. He is always helping to circulate the news of his own death."

And from Marnie Swedberg, "Exposure is the enemy's greatest weakness. As long as we believe there is no Satan, no demons and no enemy, he's got us where he wants us."

Disbelievers must ignore that the Bible refers to him 118 times under various names including Satan, Lucifer, the evil one, the devil, and the prince of this world. A consensus among theologians exists that the devil would prefer to remain unknown.

The Smell of Satan

Ted Bundy's early defense attorney Joe Aloi shared a number of eerie aspects about his client. He not only observed dramatic distortions in Bundy's face and body from time to time, but also a very unpleasant odor. During one situation Aloi claimed that "He went really nuts. I could smell him … like an animal or a wet rug." Polly Nelson served as Bundy's final lawyer before his execution. She also commented about his strange odor. Psychiatrist Dorothy Otnow Lewis, who interviewed Ted Bundy and others who encountered him, reported that a prison official in Tallahassee described an incident when: "He became weird on me." He said Bundy's body and his face would become distorted and there was an unusual odor emitting from him. Saints have assured us that evil men give off a stench that the angels cannot tolerate. It is only with the greatest difficulty that the guardian angels can keep their watch over them. There are people that live wicked lives and do horrific things.

They may escape the long arm of the law, but they will never escape the long arm of the Lord.

Padre Pio, now St. Pio, gave this testimony: "One day, while I was hearing confessions, a man came to the confessional where I was. He was tall, handsome, dressed with some refinement and he was kind and polite. He started to confess his sins, which were of every kind: against God, against man and against the morals. All the sins were obnoxious! I was disoriented, in fact for all the sins that he told me, but I responded to him with God's Word, the example of the Church, and the morals of the Saints.   But the enigmatic penitent answered me word for word, justifying his sins, always with extreme ability and politeness. He excused all the sinful actions, making them sound quite normal and natural, even comprehensible on the human level. He continued this way with the sins that were gruesome against God, Our Lady, the Saints, always using disrespectful round- about argumentation. He kept this up even with the foulest of sins that could be conjured in the mind of a most sinful man. The answers that he gave me with such skilled subtlety and malice surprised me. I wondered: who is he? What world does he come from? And I tried to look at him in order to read something on his face. At the same time, I concentrated on every word he spoke, trying to discover any clue to his identity. But suddenly; through a vivid, radiant, and internal light I clearly recognized who he was. With a sound and imperial tone, I told him: "Say long live Jesus, long live Mary!" As soon as I pronounced these sweet and powerful names, Satan instantly disappeared in a trickle of fire, leaving behind him an unbearable stench."

Stories of exorcisms frequently include inserts stating after the final demon was cast out of the person, a pungent sulfur-like smell permeated the air.

Dennis Rader told KAKE-TV reporter Larry Hatteberg during an interview in 2018 he believes a "demon" inside of him drove him to murder 10 people, including two children. "How could a guy like me, church member, raised a family, go out and do those sort of things?" Rader was a former church leader and lived at home with his wife and two children. "At some point in time, it entered me when I was young, and it basically controlled me." He thought it happened in the eighth grade and said lust and desire for fame and power drove him to murder. (Fox News/ NewsWorld and MailOnline reports).

There are three additional historical observations about Ted Bundy in support of a possible demonic influence. His birth mother Louise's younger sister Julia recalled awakening from a nap to find herself surrounded by knives from the kitchen with three-year-old Ted standing by the bed, smiling (Rule). His grandfather who Bundy said he "identified with" sometimes spoke aloud to unseen presences (Nelson).

After spending time with him, Special Agent William Hagmaier of the FBI Behavioral Analysis Unit, said he was struck by the "deep, almost mystical satisfaction" that Bundy took in murder. He added that "after a while, murder is not just a crime of lust or violence. It becomes possession" (Michaud and Aynesworth).

Nikolas Cruz told the detective about what he called a demon in his head following the Parkland massacre. He said a voice in his head told him to hurt people. The detective asked him what the demon told him to do. Cruz answered, "Burn. Kill. Destroy." Dennis Rader called himself the "BTK" Killer standing for (Bind, Torture, Kill). Were those mottoes conveyed to the killers by the voices in their heads? They are like battle cries.

Cruz said the voice was talking to him while he was there in the interrogation room, telling him to kill himself. Several times when the detective left the room, Cruz spoke to himself saying, "Kill me. Just (expletive) kill me. (expletive)." When the detective left the room again, Cruz again started talking to himself. "Why didn't he kill me?" he repeated over and over.

In the article titled "Was the Uvalde Shooter Demon-Possessed? Exorcist Exposes What May Have Happened & How We Can Respond", killer Salvador Ramos is profiled by an unnamed exorcist in the article who is Monsignor Stephen Rossetti. He said, "It is very possible that he was demonically "obsessed" and thus Satan would have a stronger sway over him. Satan fills the mind with evil thoughts. Finally, as Ramos committed himself to the act of murder, he may even have become possessed" (ABC World News Tonight with David Muir).

In Ethan Crumbley's case, prosecutors noted his hallucinations included demons

Hidden away in Dylan Klebold's journal, we find this:

"I relax on this chair — actually like a chaise — & I am talking . . . to what? I don't know — it's just there, I have the feeling that I know him, even though I consciously don't . . . & we talk like we are the same person — like he's my soul....
The everlasting contrast....
Dark. Light. God. Lucifer. Heaven. Hell. GOOD. BAD. Yes, the ever-lasting contrast. Since
existence has known the 'fight' between good & evil has continued. Obviously, this fight
can never end. Good things turn bad, bad things become good, the 'people' on the earth
see it as a battle they can win. HA f…… morons.

I get more depressed with each day . . . more Evil. . .. & I can't ever stop it!!! [illegible scribble]."

No one seems to have noted the plausible connections to the demonic in Klebold's life.

Satan and his demons do not make killers do what they do, but they plant the seeds in their minds called temptations and cultivate them to the degree the killer decides to murder people. Satan cannot force us to sin, but he can place tempting thoughts in our minds to lure us into sin because we want to be happy.

Demons are skilled observers of what we do and what we say. They use what they learn to foster and encourage temptation. They do not have to read minds to know our dirty laundry. When we give into sin, they have done their job. As Charles Kraft, an eminent anthropologist and Christian writer and speaker claimed, "Demons are like rats. They feed upon our garbage which is sin." If one wants to get rid of the demons, then they need to stop giving them the garbage of sin to feast on.

Demons can put thoughts in our minds even if they cannot read our minds. The story of Peter confronting Ananias in Acts 5:1-3 offers support for this. "Now a man named Ananias, together with his wife Sapphira, sold a piece of property. With his wife's full knowledge, he kept back part of the money for himself, but brought the rest and put it at the apostles' feet.

Then Peter said, 'Ananias, how is it that Satan has so filled your heart that you have lied to the Holy Spirit and have kept for yourself some of the money you received for the land? Didn't it belong to you before it was sold? And after it was sold, wasn't the money at your disposal? What made you think of doing such a thing? You have not lied just to human beings but to God.'"

"What made you think of doing such a thing?" That's a great question to ask our self whenever we screw up. The late comedian Flip Wilson was famous for repeatedly saying in his comedy sketches "The devil made me do it." Did the Devil make Ananias keep part of the money for himself? No, it was purely his decision, but Satan and the demons are very persistent. The Catechism of the Catholic Church states, "Sin creates a proclivity to sin; it engenders vice by repetition of the same acts" (paragraph 1865).

Sin Begins with Temptation

"Better shun the bait, than struggle in the snare" – John Dryden

Temptation in and of itself is not a sin but it can be the bait to threaten long-term goals especially like eternal life in heaven. It allures, excites, and seduces the person. From a religious standpoint, it is the inclination to engage in a short-term behavior that brings pleasure which is sinful. Hidden under the bait is a hook to one or more of the deadly sins.

St. Paul said about his experiences with temptation, "For I have the desire to do what is good, but I cannot carry it out. For what I do is not the good I want to do; no, the evil I do not want to do—this I keep on doing" (Romans 7:18-19). This admission by St. Paul is even more revealing and encouraging because it was written many years after his conversion and after he had been teaching others how to do right by Jesus' law of love. It tells us how hard it is to stay on the straight and narrow even for someone as great as St. Paul.

The world tantalizes us with things, power, lust, and honor. The key bait used by the Devil, the prince of the world, is earthly pleasure particularly connected to the flesh. The paths offered by pleasure can easily lead one into sin if the person is not careful. Our senses and emotions pull us in one direction while the mind and our conscience tug us in another direction. We are "relentlessly driven by dreams of success, some want to be rich, some want to be popular and applauded and some want power, prestige and social standing" (Vann).

The Five Physical Senses and Temptation

The human senses are on the front line in interacting with the physical world. They provide the initial channels for possible temptation and can be portals of spiritual light or darkness. What they take in is processed by the brain, filtered through the imagination and recorded in the memory. The story of Adam and Eve presents insight on how several of her senses were instrumental in Eve's fatal decision in the face of temptation. The first thing that happened is "she saw". Later, King David would do the same when "he saw" Bathsheba.

The color red is a good place to start because of its many associations with a variety of temptations and potential sins. Here are some familiar examples. You might want to match the saying with a possible connection to one or more of the "Seven Deadly Sins." Note the common thread of passion among most of them. Whether they lead to actual sinning depends on the circumstances.

Ran a red light
Red-light district
Caught red-handed
The scarlet red "A"
Red-hot mama
Red in the face
A red herring
Not worth a red cent
Better dead than red

The red-carpet treatment

Other colors have their connections to temptations too. "Green with envy" or the "Green-eyed monster." White for cleanliness, purity; black for darkness, death and evil, and so forth.

Each of the other human senses can be a gateway to temptation. The senses of smell and taste can lead to gluttony. Sense of touch can prompt lustful thoughts and sexual sin. Hearing certain trigger words can stimulate wrath, envy, and greed. One of the most dangerous temptations involving vision or sight in today's world is pornography which can lead to "cancer of the mind." "For to set the mind on the flesh is death, but to set the mind on the Spirit is life and peace" (Romans 8:6).

We move to the mind's role in dealing with temptation by focusing on our thinking.

Thinking

"The soul becomes dyed with the color of its thoughts" -
Marcus Aurelius, Meditations

Devils try to seduce the mind. All temptations are processed in the mind. Thoughts are the soft underbelly of the mind. We humans are overloaded with thousands of thoughts 24/7 because we are thinking machines. There are various estimates of how many thoughts people have in a day. Deepak Chopra, a popular New Age philosopher, put it at 60,000 to 80,000. His estimate is supported by the University of Southern California Laboratory of Neuro Imaging at 70,000. Of those many thoughts in a day, the National Science Foundation research center reported that "80% are negative." Most involve complaining about the past or what the future forebodes rather that living in the moment or the "Now" as popularized by Eckhart Tolle.

Aaron Beck, the father of cognitive behavioral therapy, found that negative thoughts fall in three categories: self, the world and the future. Negative thoughts most often involve complaining about those things that keep the mind going. Some common examples include:

I should be better than I am. (self, future)
I deserve more than I have. (self, world)
Life should be easy. (self, world, future)
The world isn't fair. (self, world)

The main focus of Beck's cognitive behavioral therapeutic approach is directed to those distorted negative thoughts that spring up spontaneously that are accepted as true that affect the individual's emotions, mood, and behavior.

Several famous authors and speakers including sales guru and motivational speaker Zig Ziglar and cognitive behavioral therapy promoter David Burns among others have used the catchy phrase Stinkin' Thinkin' to indict the rampant negative thinking that seriously messes with our emotions, moods, and life satisfaction. Stinkin' Thinkin' is a familiar phrase in 12-Step and other recovery programs and like cognitive behavioral therapy, it refers to the self-defeating tapes and scripts that continually repeat themselves in the person's mind.

Another popular catchphrase is Woulda Coulda Shoulda that is part of the book title written by Arthur Freeman which basically says that our negative thoughts about events can bother us more than the event itself. If we can change our thoughts about the event by interpreting the situation differently, then our feelings also can change.

Thoughts have transforming power. If you want to change your life, start with changing your thinking, As mentioned, Beck determined that negative thinking falls in the three categories of self, world, and future. From a Christian perspective, negative thoughts can spring up also from three sources called "the world, the flesh and the devil." The mind is connected to both the body and the soul with our physical senses, imagination and memory being again on the front lines of our vulnerability that the devils work on. However, they cannot control our will, at the inner core, which remains our "ultimate citadel of freedom and control" (Aquinas).

Devils are vigilant watchers of what we do and what we say. They use what they learn to foster and encourage temptation. They do not have to read into our minds to know our dirty laundry, rather they focus, we have learned, on the interplay between our physical sensations, visual imagery, imagination, and memory. "The devil can work on the senses of man, influence his imagination with attractive images, leading to sinful choice" (Aquinas). As Robert Wild, in writing about G. K. Chesterton, said, "The demons may tempt us in a sensual way with imaginings of false delights so that we succumb to something sinful." Note the connection once again between the senses and imaginings. We must be very careful what we let in through the senses because images lead to thoughts. As Proverbs 4:23 cautions in turn, "Be careful what you think, because your thoughts run your life."

All of us have experienced bizarre involuntary intrusive thoughts on the spare of the moment that have totally shocked, scared and amazed us. The reaction typically is, "How could I ever come up with that thought...so evil...so nasty...there must be something terribly wrong with me!" It might be impulsive bursts of profanity, wishing some people dead or imaging yourself in a triple "XXX" sexual exploit. Some impulses can be outright blasphemous or extremely violent in nature. Those instances seem to come from a very dark region deep within us. While they certainly involve negative thinking, they are not in themselves necessarily sinful unless, of course, they are acted upon.

If the person is overloaded with dark thoughts, what should they do about it?

In Romans 12:2 Saint Paul teaches,
"Do not conform to the pattern of this world but be transformed by the renewing of your mind. Then you will be able to test and approve what God's will is—his good, pleasing and perfect will."
And what is God's will for us? Our guardian angel is here to remind us that "...whatever is true, whatever is honorable, whatever is just, whatever is pure, whatever is lovely, whatever is gracious, if there is any excellence and if there is anything worthy of praise, think about these things" (Philippians 4:8). Hermas declared, "When such things make themselves felt in your heart, know that your holy angel is with you."

"One of the deepest human desires is to have one's life matter, and for people who don't believe that their lives can matter in any meaningful way begin to entertain fantasies of both revenge against society and way to be remembered forever" (Dan O'Donnell).

The killers we met did horrific, monstrous things to other people. They murdered them.

The Old Testament made it clear what our attitude back then about what their fate should be. Genesis 9:6, "Whoever sheds man's blood, by man shall his blood be shed: for in the image of God made he man." And "Whoever takes a human life shall surely be put to death" (Leviticus. 24:17).

Fifty-four percent of respondents to Gallup's annual crime survey conducted in 2021 stated that they were "in favor of the death penalty for a person convicted of murder." In 1984, eighty percent of those polled were in favor of the death penalty (Gallop News).

According to Catholic doctrine, murderers will face the "particular judgment" immediately after death to know their eternal destiny decided by the just judgment of God. It will be heaven, hell, or purgatory. We have no understanding or insight about the judgment for only God and they know. We do know they are children of God despite their despicable acts.

In his homily in the Basilica of St. Mary of the Angels at Assisi on August 4, 2016, Pope Francis said, "To offer today's world the witness of mercy is a task from which none of us can feel exempted." As Jesus said in His Sermon on the Mount, "Blessed are the merciful, for they will be shown mercy" (Matthew 5:7).

The author was taught praying for the living as well as the dead is a spiritual work of mercy no matter how bad the person was in their life because only God can judge the state of the person's soul at the time of death. While my prayers cannot help anyone who has been condemned to hell, I do not know that is where they are for sure.

As a Catholic, I believe in the existence of purgatory which means there is always the remote possibility they could be going through an extensive purification process to clean up their soul. We have no way of knowing what is in a person's heart or what they felt at their moment of death when they came face-to-face with God.

The current edition of the Catholic Catechism speaks to a change in the church's position regarding capital punishment. "Recourse to the death penalty on the part of legitimate authority, following a fair trial, was long considered an appropriate response to the gravity of certain crimes and an acceptable, albeit extreme, means of safeguarding the common good."

The change is paraphrased as follows: "Today, however, there is an increasing awareness that the dignity of the person is not lost even after the commission of very serious crimes." Due to "more effective systems of detention have been developed, which ensure the due protection of citizens but, at the same time, do not definitively deprive the guilty of the possibility of redemption" (Catholic Catechism, 2267). Life in prison provides the opportunity "of the possibility of redemption."

Returning to the Pope's homily he said, "The world needs forgiveness; too many people are caught up in resentment and harbor hatred because they are incapable of forgiving." It seems too easy to hate the murderers we met in the book. Yet, "You have heard that it was said, 'Love your neighbor and hate your enemy.' But I tell you, love your enemies and pray for those who persecute you" (Matthew 5:43-44). We are to love them? "But I say to you who hear, Love your enemies, do good to those who hate you"-Luke 6:27.

Occasionally, we will see in the media instances where family members state they are forgiving the person who murdered their loved ones.

The parents of their murdered daughter Claire chose to forgive the murderer for what he did. "My wife and I forgive Karl Pierson for what he did. We would ask all of you here (at the funeral) and all of you watching to forgive Karl Pierson. He didn't know what he was doing... Unchecked anger and rage can lead to hatred, and unchecked hatred can lead to tragedy, blindness, and a loss of humanity. The last thing Desiree [Claire's mother] and I would want is to perpetuate this anger and rage and hatred in connection with Claire. Claire would also not want this" (Rebekah L. Stratton).

A mother asked the judge for leniency for the twenty-four-year-old young man who killed her son. The judge responded, "The wellspring from which that comes, the request for mercy, is one of the greatest nobility I can imagine," he said from the bench. "It humbles me." (Megan Crepeau).

Dylann Roof shot and killed Ethel Lance one of the nine Black worshippers including the pastor after praying with them. She left five children, seven grandchildren and four great-grandchildren behind. A daughter spoke for the family. "I will never be able to hold her again. But I forgive you and have mercy on your soul," she said. "It hurts me, it hurts a lot of people, but God forgive you and I forgive you."

Jesus' message to "love one another" even our enemies is a truly difficult teaching to accept particularly if it is a murderer. It is hard to acknowledge that Dylann Roof who killed nine people is one of God's children and should receive forgiveness but that is what the guide to everlasting life teaches us to do. "Do not judge, and you will not be judged. Do not condemn, and you will not be condemned. Forgive, and you will be forgiven" (Luke 6:37).

As James Densley, a research expert on mass shooters, reminds us, "...these individuals have done horrific, monstrous things. But three days earlier, that school shooter was somebody's son, grandson, neighbor, colleague, or classmate."

There are many examples of forgiveness in the Old Testament.

Joseph's brothers planned to kill him out of envy, but God saved him. Years later the brothers came face to face with him unbeknownst he was the Pharoah's right-hand man. When he tells them who really is, they give him a message supposedly from Jacob his father who has died.

"'This is what you are to say to Joseph: I ask you to forgive your brothers the sins and the wrongs they committed in treating you so badly.' Now please forgive the sins of the servants of the God of your father." When their message came to him, Joseph wept (Genesis 50:17–21). He forgave them.

Jacob himself was forgiven by Esau after stealing Esau's birthright. He deserved to be killed for it.
"But Esau ran to meet Jacob and embraced him; he threw his arms around his neck and kissed him. And they wept" (Genesis 33:4).

As noted earlier In the New Testament, Peter came to Jesus and asked, "Lord, how many times shall I forgive my brother when he sins against me? Up to seven times?" Jesus answered, "I tell you, not seven times, but seventy-seven times." (Matthew 18:21-22). Furthermore, "...if you do not forgive others their sins, your Father will not forgive your sins" (Matthew 6:15).

The chapter heading might lead most people initially to complete the sentence "Hate the sin and **hate the sinner**!" but that is not what God wants us to do. When

Jesus was on the Cross, he fulfilled the Old Testament prophecy: "He bore the sin of many, and made intercession for the transgressors" (Isaiah 53:12) when He prayed, "Father, forgive them, for they know not what they do" (Luke 23:34) showing the merciful heart of God.

Epilogue

Mark Twain said, "What do you call love, hate, charity, revenge, humanity, magnanimity, forgiveness? Different results of the one master impulse: the necessity of securing one's self-approval."

Mass murderers seek a sense of self-worth by chasing after what Satan, the prince of the world, oversells incessantly: power, possessions, pleasure, and prestige. The murderer's actions in pursuit of the four pernicious P's leads them to violate the Fifth Commandment of "Thou shalt not kill" and brings them in mortal contact with the seven deadly sins-most of all the grave sins of pride, lust, envy, and wrath.

We have been presented with what God teaches and what grieving family members have put in practice about how we should react to a murderer.

"We must develop and maintain the capacity to forgive. He who is devoid of the power to forgive is devoid of the power to love. There is some good in the worst of us and some evil in the best of us. When we discover this, we are less prone to hate our enemies" - Martin Luther King, Jr.

"...the power to love..."

"Love one another" appears in the bible nineteen times. The most famous place is found in John 13:34 and frequently can be seen hanging in clear view on signs at sporting events as "John 13:34." The love connection most likely spawned the motto "Hate the sin and love the sinner." It does not appear anywhere in the bible, but that is what many people believe Jesus calls us to do.

If we cannot see ourselves loving a murderer, then we should at least be open to "Hate the sin and **not** hate the sinner" and leave them in God's merciful hands.

"What he has done,
is done. No prayer—
no penance—nothing—
can undo the loathsome deed,
yet he
is Yours.
And I would plead,
Lord, let him see
long and stark and clear
Your Calvary."

From the "Prayer for the Murderer" by Ruth Bell Graham.

Bibliography

Cook, Tony and Magdaleno, Johnny. "New details show interventions failed — again and again — to stop FedEx shooting," Indianapolis Star, November 16, 2021.

Crepeau, Megan. 'Justice requires truth and reconciliation': Mother of victim in Logan Square killing maintains rare outlook as son's accused killer is granted new trial," Chicago Tribune, May 31, 2022.

Cullen, Dave. "The Depressive and the Psychopath"-subtitled "At last we know why the Columbine killers did it," Slate, April 20, 2004.

Dimitropoulos, Stav. "Ted Bundy's Childhood: Lonely Boy to Window Peeper to Serial Killer," A & E, August 17, 2021.

Doughton, Sandi. "Why did Ridgway do it? Experts say he's like other serial killers," Seattle Times, November 10, 2003.

Dylan Klebold's Journal and Other Writings, Transcribed and annotated by Peter Langman.

Eric Harris' Journal and Other Writings, Transcribed and annotated by Peter Langman.

Gary, Blaine. "The Banality of Gary: A Green River Chiller". The Washington Post, April 1, 2018.

Herrero, De Santiago J, et al. "The phenomenon of serial killers from the perspective of the seven deadly sins,"

European Psychiatry, Volume 41, Supplement, April 2017.

Israelsen, Sara. "Man who shot Orem police officer apologizes, gets long prison term, "Deseret News, December2, 2005

Kravarik, Jason. "Suspect in deaths of 2 at New Mexico library called a 'hurting' youth," CNN, August 30, 2017.

Masters, Brian. The Shrine of Jeffrey Dahmer. London, England: Hodder & Stoughton. 1993.

McLean, Dorothy Cummins. "The Isla Vista Killer and the Seven Deadly Sins," The Catholic World Report, May 30, 2014.

Michaud, Stephen; Aynesworth, Hugh. The Only Living Witness: The True Story of Serial Sex Killer Ted Bundy (Paperback; revised ed.). Irving, Texas: Authorlink Press. 1999.

Nelson, Polly. Defending the Devil: My Story as Ted Bundy's Last Lawyer. New York City: William Morrow, 1994.

Nolasco, Stephaie. "BTK killer Dennis Rader tells all in unheard interview for doc: 'It's a demon that's within me'", Fox News, September 2, 2018.

O'Connell, Gerald. Pope Francis in Assisi: 'The world needs forgiveness,' America, August 04, 2016.

O'Donnell, Dan. "The Real Reason Mass Shootings Keep Happening," MacIver Institute, July 6, 2022.

Parkland School Shooter: 'A Demon Made Me Do It', CNN, August 8, 2018.

Rule, Ann. The Stranger Beside Me (Paperback; revised and updated ed.). New York City: Signet Books., 1989.

Scheff, Thomas J et al. Crime, Violence, and Self-Esteem:Review and Proposals, 1989.

Schoen, Marc. "How to Stop Violence in America," Psychology Today, October 12, 2016.

Shakhnazarova, Nika. 'IT CONTROLLED ME' Notorious BTK serial killer claims a 'demon' drove him to torture and murder 10 people in never-before-heard confession", NewsWorld News, September 3, 2018.

Silva, Jason R and Greene-Colozzi, Emily. Fame-seeking mass shooters in America: Severity, characteristics, and media coverage, Aggression and Violent Behavior, Volume 48, September–October 2019, Pages 24-35.

Stratton, Rebekah L. "Family of Victim Forgives Murderer," Prison Fellowship, January 15, 2014.

Toth, Hans. Violent Men. Chicago: Aldine Publishing Co. 1969.

Warner, Melanie. "Two Professors Found What Creates a Mass Shooter Will Politicians Pay Attention?", Politico, May 27, 2022.

Yehuda, Rachel. "How Parents' Trauma Leaves
Biological Traces in Children," Scientific American, July
1, 2022.

Other Books by the Author

Mary vs Satan: The Battle for Our Souls
The Pope and the "Sins of the Flesh"
Our Lady of Civitavecchia and the Bleeding Statue
Is God Using UFOs?
Our Mother Mary's Warnings at Civitavecchia, Akita,
Garabandal and Fatima
Why Praying at Noon Is So Important
Your Guardian Angel: Things You Maybe Didn't Know
Holy Face of Jesus Medal
Evil Really Stinks
The Many Wounds Jesus Suffered
The Power of His Holy Face for Your Life
Thanks, God for Those Close Moments
LUST: The Devil's Favorite Sin
The Devil on My Shoulder
Growing Up on Rural Route 2
Sins and God's Warning
What the Angels Have Taught Me
For People Who Are Suffering: A Treasure of Wise
Sayings
Goofy Laws Goofy World
I Bet You Are Envious Like I Am
Where the Hell Did "Hell" Go?
The Scary Warning from Garabandal
The Sacred Power of 3 O'clock Prayer
The Spiritual Power of Acronyms Workbook
Spiritual Microchips: How to Access Yours
In 2034 Anti-Christianity Triumphs in America
Am I Crazy or Just Senile?
Who Is "Angel Phanuel"?
America Doesn't Love Children
Can the Devil Read Our Minds?

Offering It Up for Souls and the World
Suffering and Spirituality: My Story

www.ingramcontent.com/pod-product-compliance
Lightning Source LLC
Chambersburg PA
CBHW071918120726
48001CB00005B/1776